The redeemed captive

returning to Zion

Or, The captivity and deliverance

Rev. John Williams

Alpha Editions

This edition published in 2019

ISBN : 9789353605384

Design and Setting By
Alpha Editions
email - alphaedis@gmail.com

THE

REDEEMED CAPTIVE

Returning to Zion

OR THE

CAPTIVITY AND DELIVERANCE

OF

REV. JOHN WILLIAMS

OF DEERFIELD

REPRINTED FROM

THE SIXTH EDITION

THE H. R. HUNTTING COMPANY

SPRINGFIELD, MASSACHUSETTS

MCMVIII

This edition is limited to 526 copies on
Mittineague paper, 26 of which are Large
Paper copies.

This volume is No...*1.6.7*...

PUBLISHERS' STATEMENT.

In this, the third volume of the INDIAN
CAPTIVITIES SERIES, the publishers have
profited by a number of valuable suggestions
and criticisms in the endeavour to improve
upon the preceding volumes of the series,
which have both been accorded much praise
alike by individuals and by the press.

As in the preceding volumes, the aim has
been to preserve as nearly as possible the
exact wording of the author, according to
the best edition obtainable. To this end,
while the book has been carefully edited,
with a number of additional explanatory
notes, the old-fashioned spellings and phrase-
ology, as well as many word-forms now
obsolete or archaic, have been left unaltered,
only palpable typographical and other minor
errors being corrected.

The Publishers desire to make the most
cordial acknowledgement of indebtedness to
Wilberforce Eames, Esq., of the New York
Public Library, who has furnished the very

valuable Bibliography by which the book
is enriched, as well as to George Sheldon,
Esq., whose careful historical introduction
adds much interest to the narrative.

The H. R. Huntting Co.,
October, 1908.

INTRODUCTION

BY

George Sheldon.

The modern student of old New England is seeking every reliable avenue which leads to, or illustrates her earlier days; and he does good service who presents to this public the kind of material to be found in this book.

"The Redeemed Captive"—the man—was a well known personage of his time, and stood out prominently during the crucial period of King William's and Queen Anne's wars. Although his standing among his fellow ministers was fairly good, yet he is better known by his trials and hardships than by his talents or attainments. He was emphatically a man of sorrows, and weighted with care, from maturity to his dying day. His peculiar experiences were not paralleled by any other man of his time. His own record of his own captivity has been and will be a much read book.

John Williams, son of Samuel, was born at Roxbury, Dec. 10, 1664. His grandfather, Robert Williams, was driven from Norwich, Eng., in 1634. Robert was a Puritan of Puritans. He brought with him his son Samuel, then an infant. Both settled in Roxbury; both were shoemakers. Samuel was a deacon in the church of the Apostle Eliot—a heritage and an environment equally good. John Williams was educated at the still famous Roxbury Latin School, and was graduated from Harvard in 1683. He was second in a class of three— all Roxbury boys. The first chapter of their lives had come to an end. When and where would the second open? For John Williams it opened Sept. 21, 1686, when he was called to be the minister of Deerfield. His cousin, William Williams, the third in his class, had been settled at Hatfield the year before, and Samuel Danforth, the first, was called to Taunton in 1687. In accordance with the custom of the times they had no training for the ministry beyond that given in the regular course at Harvard.

When young John Williams went to Deerfield, King William's war was near at hand, and Deerfield was a frontier town. The bodies as well as the souls of the minister and people were sorely tried. The cultivation of the soil, their sole reliance for a livelihood, was restricted to a narrow area, and this only when under an armed guard; with such conditions the harvest must of necessity be small and uncertain. All reserved resources soon became exhausted. There was no "base of supplies." The settlers feared actual want, and they came to feel it as a reality. To go outside the stockade for a moment unguarded was at the risk of life or liberty. But risks must be taken, or slow starvation would work its will.

The first bolt fell in June, 1693, at the north end of the Street, and ten men, women, and children were the victims. In October, a man was captured and carried

to Canada. In September, 1694, Castreen with a large
force of French and Indians from Canada, attempted
to surprise the town, but he was discovered, and the
place was successfully defended with a loss of one man
killed and two wounded. The next year a leading member of Mr. Williams' flock was ambushed and killed.
In 1696 a large family living within fifty rods of the
Meetinghouse was attacked, three of the family were
killed, two wounded and four captured. It was a Lecture day, and the people were collected in the Meetinghouse for public worship. This family was belated and
perhaps the only one outside the stockade. Three young
men were soon after carried off by swift surprise while
in the North Meadows, and the young minister himself
had a narrow escape at Broughton's Hill. The terrible
trials of these times, which minister and people bore
bravely and well, are not the theme of this book. They
seem, however, to be a fitting prelude.

    "The Redeemed Captive"—the Book—is a well
known classic of New England. Here may be found, in
fact, an epitome of the lights and shadows (flickering
indeed are the lights) during Queen Anne's war. It is
a personal, life-sized account of the New England captive in Canada. This book contains a perfect record of
a sorrowful experience of more than two and a half
years, and has no counterpart in the literature of the
period. It was written at Deerfield on the return of Mr.
Williams from captivity, and published at Boston,

March, 1706-7. It contains a narrative of the sacking of Deerfield, Feb. 29, 1703-4; the march of himself, family, and flock through three hundred miles of unbroken wilderness to Canada. It also contains a sermon preached at Boston, Dec. 5, 1706, two weeks after his arrival there from Canada.

"The Redeemed Captive" has passed through some dozen editions, the latest edited by Stephen W. Williams, M. D., in 1853. A third edition, commonly called the "Prince edition," was published in Boston, 1758. This included a valuable appendix by Rev. Stephen Williams, D. D., of Longmeadow, himself a "Boy Captive." In 1795 this edition was faithfully reproduced by Rev. John Taylor of Deerfield, with an appendix by himself which contains a brief account of the Indian depredations in the Valley until the conquest of Canada. This is called the "Taylor edition." It is on the whole the most satisfactory edition which we have met with. It is this which is now presented to the public in a new dress. "The Redeemed Captive" was also published at Greenfield, 1800, in connection with Robert Breck's Century Sermon, preached at Springfield, 1775; and again in connection with the Narrative of Mary Rowlandson, at Brookfield, in 1811.

In a recently published book concerning the early days of John Williams, there may be found, it is said, "the most complete, accurate and interesting account of life in the Bay Colony during its first half century." In

"The Redeemed Captive" those interested in the life of that period may find opportunity to compare this half century with the half century which followed.

Mr. Williams was a striking example of the Puritan life in thought and action. He lived and walked in the faith enjoined by the theology of the day—hard and narrow enough to our eyes, and utterly lacking in charity. Indeed, he was taught by his townsman, Gov. Thomas Dudley, that toleration was an abomination and a sin. To modern minds the Deity worshipped under this theology seems a tangled mass of contradictions. To define it in common terms would seem to Mr. Williams irreverent and sacrilegious. He believed that the Scripture with all its contradictions and crudities was the language of God, from the first word to the last. As it declared that man was made in the image of God, he could not escape the conception that God was a personal being, with a mind like unto his own, but with unlimited power for good or evil. Mr. Williams believed also that this Being was at enmity with man, and had doomed the whole race to eternal woe; that this was a well deserved sentence from which there was no escape save by softening the heart of the Deity by an appeal to His human side. To this end there was constant worship and ascribing to Him all honor and power and glory. He did not realize that the laws of Nature, by whatever name called, were unchangeable. He believed the laws of Nature had been changed upon his own petition. He records in this volume, that when in unusual straits he had petitioned for relief, there had been in response a change in the weather. He believed that the duty of man to God was fully revealed in the Scripture. He might have known, and no one will question the fact, that this "revelation" has been read a thousand ways, and that the disagreements have filled the Christian world with misery and woe; that millions of men, women, and children have been butchered, and their homes turned to ashes in consequence of this disagreement. What kind of a *revelation* is this!

John Williams was good, brave, honest, and played well his part. He must be judged by his own time. He did not formulate the Deity he trusted and worshipped. Many doubt if such a Deity could have been formulated this side of the Dark Ages.

No thinking person can read this book without a feeling of thankfulness that he is living in an age when the barbarian no longer terrorizes the land, and when the nightmare of superstition is passing away in the new light of Science.

BIBLIOGRAPHY

1707.

The Redeemed Captive Returning ‖ to Zion.‖ A Faithful History ‖ of ‖ Remarkable Occurrences, ‖ in the ‖ Captivity ‖ and the ‖ Deliverance ‖ of ‖ Mr. John Williams; ‖ Minister of the Gospel, in Deerfield, ‖ Who, in the Desolation which befel that ‖ Plantation, by an Incursion of the French ‖ & Indians, was by Them carried away, ‖ with his Family, and his Neighbourhood, ‖ unto Canada. ‖ Whereto there is annexed a Sermon ‖ Preached by him, upon his Return, at ‖ the Lecture in Boston, Decemb. 5, 1706. ‖ On those Words, Luk. 8, 39. Return to thine ‖ own House, and shew how great Things God ‖ hath done unto thee. ‖ *Boston in N. E. Printed by B. Green, for ‖ Samuel Phillips, at the Brick Shop,* 1707. ‖ 8 vo., pp. (6), 104.

NOTE. The Narrative of Williams's Captivity ends on page 87, on the verso of which is the following title of the Sermon:—Reports of Divine Kindness: ‖ or, ‖ Remarkable Mercies ‖ Should be Faithfully Published, ‖ For the Praise of ‖ God ‖ the Giver. ‖ Set forth in a Sermon Preached at ‖ Boston Lecture, Decemb. 5, 1706. ‖ By John Williams, ‖ Pastor of the Church of Christ in Deerfield; ‖ Soon after his Return from a doleful Captivity. ‖ . . . ‖ *Boston: Printed for S. Phillips, at the Brick Shop,* 1707. ‖ The Sermon fills pp. 89-104.

Copies:—American Antiquarian Society, Worcester, Mass.; Harvard College Library, Cambridge, Mass.;

Massachusetts Historical Society, Boston, Mass.; John
Carter Brown Library, Providence, R. I.   Brinley's copy
sold in 1879 for $106.

1720.

The Second Edition. ‖ *Boston:* ‖ *Printed by T. Fleet, for
Samuel Phillips, at the* ‖ *Three Bibles and Crown in King
Street*, 1720. ‖ 8 vo, pp. (6), 98.

NOTE. This edition contains only the Narrative of the
Captivity, the Sermon not being reprinted.
Copies:—New York Public Library (Lenox collec-
tion.)

1758.

The Third Edition. ‖ As also an Appendix: Containing
an Account ‖ of those taken Captive at Deerfield, February 29, 1703, 4. ‖ of those kill'd after they went out of
Town, those who ‖ returned, and of those still absent
from their native Country; ‖ of those who were Slain at
that Time in or near the Town; ‖ and of the Mischief
done by the Enemy in Deerfield, from ‖ the Beginning
of its Settlement to the Death of the Rev. Mr. ‖ Williams,
in 1729. With a Conclusion to the whole. ‖ By the Rev.
Mr. Williams of Springfield, and the Rev. ‖ Mr. Prince
of Boston. ‖ *Boston: Printed and Sold by S. Kneeland,* ‖
opposite the Probate-Office in Queen-street, 1758. ‖ 8 vo,
pp. (4) IV, 104.

NOTE. This edition begins with a half-title:—A ‖ Faithful Narrative ‖ of ‖ Remarkable Occurrences ‖ In the Captivity of the Reverend ‖ Mr. John Williams, &c. ‖
The Narrative ends on page 77. The Sermon, *Reports of Divine Kindness*, with title-page dated 1758, fills pp. 79-94. The Appendix, pp. 95-104, is dated Boston, Dec. 20, 1757, and signed T. Prince.
Copies:—Boston Public Library (Prince Collection); New York Public Library (Lenox Collection).

1773

The Fourth Edition. ‖ . . . ‖ *Boston: Printed.* ‖ *New-London: Re-printed by T. Green.* ‖ [1773.] 8 vo, pp. 79.

NOTE. The Narrative ends on page 58, and is followed on the next page by the title-page of the Sermon, *Reports of Divine Kindness*, which has the imprint, with date:— *New-London:* ‖ *Re-printed and sold by T. Green.* 1773. ‖ This edition, according to Dr. Trumbull (Brinley catalogue, no. 497), was advertised by the printer, as "just published," in April, 1773. It is a reprint of the 1758 edition, including the Appendix. See also Trumbull's *List of Books printed in Connecticut*, no. 1670.
Copies:—New York Public Library (Lenox collection), lacking pp. 77-79.

1774

The Fifth Edition. ‖ . . . ‖ *Boston:* ‖ *Printed and Sold by John Boyle next door to the Three* ‖ *Doves in Marlborough-Street.* 1774. ‖ 8 vo., pp. 70.

Note.   The Narrative in this edition ends on page 52,
the Sermon entitled *Reports of Divine Kindness* follow-
ing with imprint, *Boston:* || *Printed and Sold by John
Boyle in Marlborough-Street.* || MDCCLXXIV. || Reprint
of the 1773 edition, with the Appendix.

Copies:—Library of Congress; Massachusetts Historical Society.

1776

The Fifth Edition. || . . . || *Boston: Printed.* || *New-
London: Re-printed by T. Green.* || [1776.] 8 vo, pp. 72.

Note.   In this edition the Narrative ends on page 56,
followed on pp. 57-66 by the sermon, *Reports of Divine
Kindness,* with dated imprint, *New-London:* || *Re-printed
and Sold by T. Green.* 1776. || The Appendix fills pp. 67-72.

Dr. Trumbull in the Brinley Catalogue, nos. 500 and
5577, describes two copies of "The Fifth Edition," with
imprint, *New London, reprinted, T. Green,* n. d. [1780 ?],
which are without doubt the same as the above, he having
probably overlooked the imprint date on page 57.   In
fact, one of these two copies, no. 5577, which lacks the
Appendix, is now in Yale University Library, and contains the date 1776 on the second title.

Copies:—Library of Congress; Yale University Library.

1793

Annexed to which, is a || Sermon, || Preached by him
upon his return. || Also, || An Appendix, || By the Rev.

Mr. Williams, of Springfield. || Likewise, || An Appendix, || By the Rev. Mr. Taylor, of Deerfield. || With a Conclusion to the whole, || By the Rev. Mr. Prince, of Boston. || The Fourth Edition, with Additions. || *Printed at Greenfield, Massachusetts.* || *By Thomas Dickman.* || MDCCXCIII. || 12 mo., pp. (2), iii, 154.

NOTE. Reprinted from the 1758 edition. Mr. Taylor's Appendix, pp. 121-151, contains an account "of the mischief done by the enemy, in Deerfield, and its vicinity," from 1745 to 1749 and from 1755 to 1759, closing with a circumstantial account of the Fall Fight, in May, 1676.

Copies:—Massachusetts Historical Society; New York Public Library (Lenox collection).

1795

The Sixth Edition. || *Printed by Samuel Hall, No. 53, Cornhill, Boston.* || 1795. || 12 mo, pp. 132.

NOTE. A reprint of the edition of 1793, with Mr. Taylor's Appendix.

Copies:—Library of Congress; Massachusetts Historical Society; New York Public Library (Lenox collection).

1800 [or 1802]

Subjoined to this is, || A Sermon, || delivered in the First Parish in Spring- || field, on the 16th of October, 1775. || Just one hundred years from the burn- || ing of the town by the Indians. || By Robert Breck, A. M. || Pastor of the Church there. ‖ The Sixth Edition, with Additions. ‖ *Printed and sold at Greenfield, Mass. by* ‖ *Thomas Dickman,* ‖ MDCCC. ‖ 12 mo, pp. 248.

NOTE. Although dated 1800 on the title page, this edition was perhaps really printed in 1802, if the date of Mr. Taylor's note, as given below, is correct. It is the most complete, in the way of Appendixes, of all the editions, as it contains on pp. 197-220 an "Historical Sketch of Deerfield," from 1669 to 1799, apparently not printed elsewhere, to which is prefixed this note:—

"Mr. Dickman, Sir, Agreeably to your request, I send you the following extracts from a discourse, delivered at Deerfield, on the first day of the present century. As you wish to annex these to my former appendix to Mr. Williams's narrative, it may be necessary to observe, that some parts of the historical sketch I have given of Deerfield, is drawn from the narrative itself.—Yet as there are circumstances, which Mr. Williams omitted; I send you what I have written upon these events, without any material alterations. John Taylor. Deerfield, Jan. 1st, 1802."

The narrative of captivity ends on p. 125; Williams's Sermon on Dec. 5, 1706, fills pp. 127-148; Mr. Stephen Williams's Appendix, pp. 149-158; Rev. John Taylor's Appendix, pp. 159-197; Mr. T. Prince's Observations, pp. 220-224. Then follows Breck's Century Sermon, pp. 225-248, first published at Hartford in 1784, and reprinted here with the following title:—"Past Dispensations of Providence called to Mind. In a Sermon, delivered in the First Parish in Springfield, on the 16th of October

1775. Just one hundred years from the burning of the town by the Indians. By Robert Breck, A. M. Pastor of the Church there."
Copies:—American Antiquarian Society.

1802

New-Haven: Printed by William W. Morse. || 1802. || 12 mo, pp. 188.

NOTE. Reprinted from the edition of 1793 or 1795, with Mr. Taylor's first Appendix.
Copies:—American Antiquarian Society; Boston Public Library; Massachusetts Historical Society.

1811

The || Captivity and Deliverance || of || Mr. John Williams, || Pastor of the Church in Deerfield, || and || Mrs. Mary Rowlandson, || of Lancaster, || who were taken, together with their families || and neighbors, by the French and Indians, || and carried into Canada. || Written by Themselves. || *Brookfield,* || *Printed by Hori Brown,* || *From the press of E. Merriam & Co.* || *September—*1811. || 12 mo, pp. 116; Mrs. Rowlandson's Captivity, pp. 80.

NOTE. This edition contains only the narrative of captivity, followed on pp. 111-116, by a notice of Mr. Williams's death in 1729, "From the Weekly News Letter No. 130, and the Weekly Journal No. 118." Mrs. Rowlandson's narrative has a separate title, with imprint as in the first title:—"The || Captivity and Deliverance || of || Mrs.

Mary Rowlandson, ‖ of Lancaster, ‖ who was taken by the French and Indians, ‖ Written by Herself."
Copies:—American Antiquarian Society.

1832

The ‖ Deerfield Captive, ‖ an ‖ Indian Story; ‖ being a ‖ Narrative of Facts, ‖ for ‖ the instruction of the young. ‖ *A. Phelps,* ‖ *Greenfield, Mass.* ‖ 1832. ‖ Square 18mo, pp. 68 and printed covers.

NOTE. By the Rev. Titus Strong, D. D., but published anonymously. It was copyrighted in 1831, and the prefatory note is dated Greenfield, Sept. 10, 1831. The frontispiece is a view of the old house in Deerfield which escaped the conflagration in 1704. The cover-title reads:—"The Deerfield Captive, ‖ an interesting Indian Story; being a narrative ‖ of facts, ‖ for the instruction of the young. ‖ [Picture.] ‖ *Greenfield:* ‖ *Published by A. Phelps.*"

1833

The ‖ Redeemed Captive : ‖ a Narrative ‖ of the ‖ Captivity, Sufferings, and Return ‖ of the ‖ Rev. John Williams, ‖ minister of Deerfield, Massachusetts, ‖ who was taken prisoner by the Indians ‖ on the destruction of the ‖ town, A. D. 1704. ‖ For Sabbath Schools. ‖ *New-York: Published by S. W. Benedict & Co.* ‖ *Evangelist Office, No. 20, Ann St.* ‖ 1833. ‖ 24 mo, pp. 116. Frontispiece of the old house at Deerfield, and plate of captives in a canoe, facing p. 24.

NOTE. Written in the form of letters by Rev. Joshua Leavitt, whose name appears in the copyright notice, and first published in the *New-York Evangelist*, in February and March, 1833. An appendix of historical documents fills pp. 89-116.

1834

The || Deerfield Captive. || An || Indian Story; || being a || Narrative of Facts, || for || the instruction of the young. || Second Edition. || *A. Phelps,* || *Greenfield, Mass.* || 1834. || Square 18 mo, pp. 68, last page misnumbered 78, and printed covers.

NOTE. A reprint of the edition of 1832, with two additional woodcuts.

1837

The || Deerfield Captive, || an || Indian Story; || being a || Narrative of Facts, || for the || instruction of the young. || Third Edition. || *A. Phelps,* || *Greenfield, Mass.* || 1837. || Square 18 mo, pp. 68 and printed covers.

1837

A || Biographical Memoir || of the || Rev. John Williams, || First Minister of Deerfield, Massachusetts. || With a slight sketch of ancient Deerfield, and || and [sic] an account of the Indian Wars in that || place and vicinity. || With an appendix, containing the journal of the ||

Rev. Doctor Stephen Williams, ‖ of Longmeadow, during his captivity, ‖ and other papers relating to the early ‖ Indian Wars in Deerfield. ‖ By Stephen W. Williams, A. M.; M. D. ‖ Honorary member of the New York Historical Society, &c. &c. ‖ Author of the Catechism of Medical Jurisprudence, &c. &c. ‖ *Greenfield, Mass.* ‖ *Published and printed by C. J. J. Ingersoll* ‖ 1837 ‖ 12 mo, pp. 127.

NOTE. "The Redeemed Captive . . has been out of print for more than twenty years. The demand for that work has been great for a long time, and I have been induced to prepare another edition of it, in a new form, under the title of a Biographical Memoir of the pious and distinguished author of that work, in which I have thrown out much which has appeared to me extraneous, and have added many particulars in relation to his life and character which have never before been published. The whole of it, except the extracts, is in my own language."— *Preface.*

1841

Memoir of ‖ Rev. John Williams, ‖ the Deerfield Captive, ‖ with sketches of ‖ Early Indian Wars. ‖ *Greenfield, Mass.* ‖ 1841. ‖ 12 mo, pp. 127.

NOTE. Title-label as above pasted on outside of front cover. Inside title is dated 1837, and is identical with the edition described under that date, this being merely a reissue.

1853

The || Redeemed Captive returning to Zion: || or, || a || faithful history of remarkable || occurrences || in the Captivity and Deliverance || of || Mr. John Williams, || Minister of the Gospel in Deerfield, || who in the desolation which befel that plantation by || an incursion of the French and Indians, was by them || carried away, with his family and his neighbor- || hood, into Canada, || drawn up by himself. || To which is added, || a biographical memoir of the || Reverend Author, || with || an appendix and notes, || by || Stephen W. Williams, A. M., M. D. || Honorary Member of the New York Historical Society, Corresponding || Member of the National Institute, etc., etc. || *Northampton:* || *Hopkins, Bridgman, and Company.* || 1853. || 12 mo, pp. 192. Frontispiece, *View of the old house in Deerfield which escaped the conflagration in 1704;* portrait, facing p. 144, of *Stephen Williams, D. D.*

1884

The || Deerfield Captive, || an || Indian Story; || being a || Narrative of Facts, || for || the instruction of the young. || Written by Rev. Titus Strong, D. D. || *A. Phelps;* || *Greenfield, Mass.* || 1834. *Third Edition,* reprinted by *F. G. Tilton & Co., Greenfield, Mass.* || 1884. || Square 18 mo, pp. 63, and printed covers. Frontispiece of Memorial Stone erected by the Pocumtuck Valley Memorial Association, Aug. 12, 1884.

NOTE. This is really the fourth edition, although wrongly numbered the third.

1899

New Tracks in an Old Trail. ‖ By George Sheldon. ‖ (Read at P. V. M. A. meeting at Memorial hall, Old Deerfield, Feb. 28, 1899.) ‖ [n. p. 1899.] 8 vo, pp. 11, in double columns.

NOTE. A critical examination of "The Redeemed Captive" of Parson John Williams and the "Journal" of his son Stephen.

The DEDICATION.

To his Excellency

JOSEPH DUDLEY, Esq.

Captain-General, and Governor in Chief, in and over her Majesty's Province of the Massachusetts-Bay in New-England, &c.

Sir,

It was a satyrical answer, and deeply re-proachful to mankind, which the philosopher gave to that question, *What soonest grows old?* Replied, *Thanks.* The reproach of it would not be so sensible, were there not sensible demonstrations of the truth of it, in those that wear the character of the ingenuous. Such as are at first surprised at, and seem to have no common relish of divine goodness, yet too soon lose the impression: They sang God's

praise,

praise, but soon forgat his works. That it should be thus with respect to our benefactors on earth, is contrary to the ingenuity of human nature; but that our grateful resentments of the signal favours of Heaven should soon be worn off by time, is, to the last degree criminal and unpardonable.

It would be unaccountable stupidity in me, not to maintain the most lively and awful sense of divine rebukes, which the holy God has seen meet, in spotless sovereignty, to dispense to me, my family and people, in delivering us into the hands of those that hated us; who led us into a strange land. My soul has these still in remembrance, and is humbled in me. However, God has given us plentiful occasion to sing of mercy as well as judgment. The wonders of divine mercy, which we have seen in the land of our captivity, and deliverance therefrom, cannot be forgotten without incurring the guilt of the blackest ingratitude.

To preserve the memory of these, it has been thought adviseable to publish a short
account

account of some of those signal appearances of divine power and goodness for us; hoping it may serve to excite the praise, faith and hope of all that love God; and may peculiarly serve to cherish a grateful spirit, and to render the impressions of God's mighty works indelible on my heart, and on those who with me have seen the wonders of the Lord, and tasted of his salvation; that we may not fall under that heavy charge made against Israel of old, Psal. lxxviii. 11, 42. *They forgat his works, and the wonders he shewed them: They remembered not his hand, nor the day that he delivered them from the enemy.*

And I cannot, Sir, but think it most agreeable to my duty to God, our supreme redeemer, to mention your Excellency's name with honour; since Heaven has honoured you as the prime instrument in returning our captivity. Sure I am, the laws of justice and gratitude (which are the laws of God) do challenge from us the most publick acknowledgments of your uncommon sympathy with us, your children,

in

in our bonds, expressed in all endearing methods of parental care and tenderness. All your people are cherished under your wings, happy in your government, and are obliged to bless God for you: And among your people, those who are immediately exposed to the outrages of the enemy, have peculiarly felt refreshment from the benign influences of your wise and tender conduct; and are under the most sensible engagements to acknowledge your Excellency, under God, as the breath of their nostrils.

Your uncommon sagacity and prudence, in contriving to loose the bonds of your captived children; your unwearied vigour and application, in pursuing them, to work our deliverance, can never be enough praised. It is most notorious, that nothing was thought too difficult by you to effect this design, in that you readily sent your own son, Mr. William Dudley, to undergo the hazards and hardships of a tedious voyage, that this affair might be transacted with success; which must not be
                                        forgotten,

forgotten, as an expression of your great so-
licitude and zeal to recover us from the
tyranny and oppression of our captivity.

I doubt not but that the God, whom herein
you have served, will remember, and gloriously reward you; and may Heaven long preserve you at our helm, a blessing so necessary
for the tranquility of this province, in this dark
and tempestuous season. May the best of
blessings, from the Father of Lights, be show-
ered down upon your person, family and government; which shall be the prayer of
Your Excellency's most humble
obedient, and dutiful servant,
JOHN WILLIAMS.
March 3, 1706,7.

THE

REDEEMED CAPTIVE

RETURNING TO

Z I O N .

THE history I am going to write, proves,
that days of fasting and prayer, without
reformation, will not avail to turn away the
anger of God from a professing people; and
yet witnesseth, how very advantageous, gracious supplications are, to prepare particular
Christians, patiently to suffer the will of God,
in very trying publick calamities. For some
of us, moved with fear, set apart a day of
prayer, to ask of God, either to spare, and
save us from the hands of our enemies, or to
prepare us to sanctify and honour him in what
way

way soever he should come forth towards us.
The places of Scripture from whence we were
entertained, were Gen. xxxii. 10, 11. *I am
not worthy of the least of all the mercies, and
of all the truth which thou hast shewed unto
thy servant. Deliver me, I pray thee, from the
hand of my brother, from the hand of Esau:
For I fear him, lest he will come and smite me,
and the mother with the children.* [In the forenoon.] And Gen. xxxii. 26. *And he said,
let me go, for the day breaketh: And he said, I
will not let thee go, except thou bless me.* [In
the afternoon.] From which we were called
upon to spread the causes of fear, relating to
our own selves, or families, before God; as
also, how it becomes us, with an undeniable
importunity, to be following God, with earnest prayers for his blessing, in every condition. And it is very observable, how God ordered our prayers, in a peculiar manner, to
be going up to him; to prepare us, with a right
Christian spirit, to undergo, and endure
suffering trials.

Not

Not long after, the holy and righteous God brought us under great trials, as to our persons and families, which put us under a necessity of spreading before him, in a wilderness, the distressing dangers and calamities of our relations; yea, that called on us, notwithstanding seeming present frowns, to resolve by his grace not to be sent away without a blessing. Jacob, in wrestling, has the hollow of his thigh put out of joint; and it is said to him, *Let me go;* yet he is rather animated to an heroical, Christian resolution to continue earnest for the blessing, than discouraged from asking.

ON the twenty-ninth of February, 1703,4, not long before the break of day, the enemy came in like a flood upon us; our watch being unfaithful, an evil, whose awful effects, in a surprisal of our fort, should bespeak all watchmen to avoid, as they would not bring the charge of blood upon themselves. They came to my house in the beginning of the onset, and
by

by their violent endeavours to break open door
and windows, with axes and hatchets, awaked
me out of sleep; on which I leaped out of bed,
and running toward the door, perceived the
enemy making their entrance into the house.
I called to awaken two soldiers, in the chamber; and returned toward my bed-side, for my
arms. The enemy immediately brake into
the room, I judge to the number of twenty,
with painted faces, and hideous acclamations.
I reached up my hands to the bed-tester, for
my pistol, uttering a short petition to God, for
everlasting mercies for me and mine, on the
account of the merits of our glorified Redeemer; expecting a present passage through
the valley of the shadow of death; saying in
myself, as Isaiah xxxviii. 10, 11. *I said, in
the cutting off of my days, I shall go to the
gates of the grave: I am deprived of the residue
of my years. I said, I shall not see the Lord,
even the Lord, in the land of the living: I shall
behold man no more with the inhabitants of the
world.* Taking down my pistol, I cocked it,
and

and put it to the breast of the first Indian who came up; but my pistol missing fire, I was seized by three Indians, who disarmed me, and bound me naked, as I was in my shirt, and so I stood for near the space of an hour. Binding me, they told me they would carry me to Quebec. My pistol missing fire was an occasion of my life's being preserved; since which I have also found it profitable to be crossed in my own will. The judgment of God did not long slumber against one of the three which took me, who was a captain, for by sun-rising he received a mortal shot from my next neighbour's house; who opposed so great a number of French and Indians as three hundred, and yet were no more than seven men in an ungarrisoned house.

I cannot relate the distressing care I had for my dear wife, who had lain-in but a few weeks before, and for my poor children, family, and Christian neighbours. The enemy fell to rifling the house, and entered in great numbers into every room of the house. I begged
of

of God to remember mercy in the midst of
judgment; that he would so far restrain their
wrath, as to prevent their murdering of us;
that we might have grace to glorify his name,
whether in life or death; and, as I was able,
committed our state to God. The enemies
who entered the house were all of them Indians and Macquas*, insulted over me a while,
holding up hatchets over my head, threatening
to burn all I had; but yet God, beyond expec-
tation, made us in a great measure to be pitied;
for though some were so cruel and barbarous as to take and carry to the door, two
of my children, and murder them, as also a
negro woman; yet they gave me liberty to put
on my clothes, keeping me bound with a cord
on one arm, till I put on my clothes to the
other; and then changing my cord, they let
me

* The attacking party consisted, according to French accounts,
of 50 Canadians and 200 Abenaki and Caughnawaga Indians.
The Caughnawagas, who were formerly called also *Maquas* or
Macquas, were converted Mohawk Indians from New York who,
induced by the French Jesuit missionaries to remove to Canada,
settled at St. Louis, or *Caughnawaga*, on the right bank of the St.
Lawrence, a little above Montreal, where their descendents still
remain.

me dress myself, and then pinioned me again:
Gave liberty to my dear wife to dress herself,
and our children. About sun an hour high,
we were all carried out of the house, for a
march, and saw many of the houses of my
neighbours in flames, perceiving the whole
fort, one house excepted, to be taken. Who
can tell what sorrows pierced our souls, when
we saw ourselves carried away from God's
sanctuary, to go into a strange land, exposed
to so many trials ? The journey being at least
three hundred miles we were to travel ; the
snow up to the knees, and we never inured
to such hardships and fatigues; the place we
were to be carried to, a popish country. Upon
my parting from the town, they fired my house
and barn. We were carried over the river, to
the foot of the mountain, about a mile from
my house, where we found a great number of
our Christian neighbours, men, women and
children, to the number of an hundred, nine-
teen of whom were afterwards murdered by
the way, and two starved to death, near
                                    Cowass,

Cowass, in a time of great scarcity or famine, the savages underwent there. When we came to the foot of the mountain, they took away our shoes, and gave us, in the room of them, Indian shoes, to prepare us for our travel. Whilst we were there, the English beat out a company, that remained in the town, and pursued them to the river, killing and wounding many of them, but the body of the army, being alarmed, they repulsed those few English that pursued them.

I am not able to give you an account of the number of the enemy slain; but I observed after this fight, no great insulting mirth, as I expected; and saw many wounded persons, and for several days together they buried of their party, and one of chief note among the Macquas. The governour of Canada told me, his army had that success with the loss of but eleven men, three Frenchmen, one of whom was the lieutenant of the army, five Macquas, and three Indians: But after my arrival at Quebec, I spake with an Englishman, who was

was taken the last war, and married there, and of their religion; who told me, they lost above forty, and that many were wounded. I replied, the governour of Canada said they lost but eleven men. He answered, it is true, that there were but eleven killed out-right at the taking of the fort, but that many others were wounded, among whom was the ensign of the French; but, said he, they had a fight in the meadow, and that in both engagements they lost more than forty. Some of the soldiers, both French and Indians, then present, told me so, (said he), adding, that the French always endeavour to conceal the number of their slain.

After this, we went up the mountain, and saw the smoke of the fires in town, and beheld the awful desolations of Deerfield: And before we marched any farther, they killed a sucking child of the English. There were slain by the enemy, of the inhabitants of our town, to the number of thirty-eight, besides nine of the neighbouring towns. We
travelled

travelled not far the first day; God made the
heathen so to pity our children, that though
they had several wounded persons of their
own to carry upon their shoulders for thirty
miles, before they came to the river, yet they
carried our children, incapable of travelling,
upon their shoulders, and in their arms. When
we came to our lodging place, the first night,
they dug away the snow, and made some wigwams, cut down some of the small branches
of spruce trees to lie down on, and gave the
prisoners somewhat to eat; but we had but
little appetite. I was pinioned, and bound
down that night, and so I was every night
whilst I was with the army. Some of the
enemy who brought drink with them from the
town, fell to drinking, and in their drunken
fit they killed my negro man, the only dead
person I either saw at the town, or in the way.
In the night an Englishman made his escape.
In the morning I was called for, and ordered by
the general to tell the English, that if any
more made their escape, they would burn
the

the rest of the prisoners. He that took me was unwilling to let me speak with any of the prisoners, as we marched; but on the morning of the second day, he being appointed to guard the rear, I was put into the hands of my other master, who permitted me to speak to my wife, when I overtook her, and to walk with her, to help her in her journey. On the way we discoursed of the happiness of those who had a right to an house not made with hands, eternal in the heavens; and God for a father, and friend; as also, that it was our reasonable duty, quietly to submit to the will of God, and to say, the will of the Lord be done. My wife told me her strength of body began to fail, and that I must expect to part with her; saying, she hoped God would preserve my life, and the life of some, if not all of our children, with us; and commended to me, under God, the care of them. She never spake any discontented word as to what had befallen us, but with suitable expressions justified God in what had befallen us. We soon made an

halt,

halt, in which time my chief surviving master came up, upon which I was put upon marching with the foremost, and so made to take my last farewell of my dear wife, the desire of my eyes, and companion in many mercies and afflictions. Upon our separation from each other, we asked for each other, grace sufficient for what God should call us to. After our being parted from one another, she spent the few remaining minutes of her stay in reading the holy Scriptures; which she was wont personally every day to delight her soul in reading, praying, meditating of, and over, by herself, in her closet, over and above what she heard out of them in our family worship. I was made to wade over a small river, and so were all the English, the water above knee-deep, the stream very swift; and after that, to travel up a small mountain; my strength was almost spent, before I came to the top of it. No sooner had I overcome the difficulty of that ascent, but I was permitted to sit down, and be unburthened of my pack. I

sat

sat pitying those who were behind, and in-
treated my master to let me go down, and help
up my wife; but he refused, and would not
let me stir from him. I asked each of the
prisoners (as they passed by me) after her,
and heard that in passing through the above-
said river, she fell down, and was plunged
over head and ears in the water; after
which she traveled not far; for at the
foot of this mountain, the cruel and blood-
thirsty savage, who took her, slew her with his
hatchet, at one stroke; the tidings of which
were very awful; and yet such was the hard-
heartedness of the adversary, that my tears
were reckoned to me as a reproach. My loss,
and the loss of my children, was great; our
hearts were so filled with sorrow, that nothing
but the comfortable hopes of her being taken
away in mercy to herself, from the evils we
were to see, feel, and suffer under, (and joined
to the assembly of the spirits of just men
made perfect, to rest in peace, and joy un-
speakable, and full of glory, and the good
pleasure

pleasure of God thus to exercise us), could have kept us from sinking under, at that time. That Scripture, Job i. 21. *Naked came I out of my mother's womb, and naked shall I return thither; the Lord gave, and the Lord hath taken away, blessed be the name of the Lord;* was brought to my mind, and from it, that an afflicting God was to be glorified; with some other places of Scripture, to persuade to a patient bearing my afflictions.

We were again called upon to march, with a far heavier burden on my spirits, than on my back. I begged of God, to over-rule, in his providence, that the corpse of one so dear to me, and of one whose spirit he had taken to dwell with him in glory, might meet with a Christian burial, and not be left for meat to the fowls of the air, and beasts of the earth: A mercy that God graciously vouchsafed to grant: For God put it into the hearts of my neighbours to come out as far as she lay, to take up her corpse, recarry it to the town, and decently to bury it, soon after. In our march they

they killed another sucking infant of one of my neighbours; and before night, a girl, of about eleven years of age. I was made to mourn at the consideration of my flock's being so far a flock of slaughter, many being slain in the town, and so many murdered in so few miles from the town; and from fears what we must yet expect from such who delightfully imbrued their hands in the blood of so many of his people. When we came to our lodging place, an Indian captain from the eastward spake to my master about killing of me, and taking off my scalp. I lifted up my heart to God, to implore his grace and mercy in such a time of need; and afterwards I told my master, if he intended to kill me, I desired he would let me know of it, assuring him that my death, after a promise of quarter, would bring the guilt of blood upon him. He told me he would not kill me. We laid down and slept, for God sustained and kept us. In the morning we were all called before the chief sachems of the Macquas and Indians,

that

that a more equal distribution might be made
of the prisoners among them. At my going
from the wigwam, my best clothing was taken
away from me. As I came nigh the place appointed, some of the captives met me, and told
me, they thought the enemies were going to
burn some of us, for they had peeled off
the bark from several trees, and acted very
strangely. To whom I replied, they could act
nothing against us, but as they were permitted
of God, and I was persuaded he would prevent such severities. When we came to the
wigwam appointed, several of the captives
were taken from their former masters, and
put into the hands of others: But I was sent
again to my two masters, who brought me
from my house.

In our fourth day's march, the enemy killed
another of my neighbours, who being near the
time of travail, was wearied with her journey.
When we came to the great river, the enemy
took sleighs to draw their wounded, several
of our children, and their packs; and marched

a

a great pace. I travelled many hours in water up to the ankles. Near night I was very lame, having before my travel wrenched my ankle-bone and sinews. I thought, so did others, that I should not be able to hold out to travel far. I lifted up my heart to God (my only refuge) to remove my lameness, and carry me through with my children and neighbours, if he judged it best. However, I desired God would be with me in my great change, if he called me by such a death to glorify him; and that he would take care of my children and neighbours, and bless them; and within a little space of time, I was well of my lameness, to the joy of my children and neighbours, that saw so great an alteration in my travelling.

On the Saturday, the journey was long and tedious; we travelled with such speed, that four women were tired, and then slain by them who led them captive.

On the Sabbath day we rested, and I was permitted to pray and preach to the captives. The

The place of Scripture spoken from, was Lam. i. 18. *The Lord is righteous, for I have rebelled against his commandment: Hear, I pray you, all people, and behold my sorrow: My virgins and my young men are gone into captivity.* The enemy, who said to us, sing us one of Zion's songs, were ready, some of them, to upbraid us, because our singing was not so loud as theirs. When the Macquas and Indians were chief in power, we had this revival in our bondage; to join together in the worship of God, and encourage one another to a patient bearing the indignation of the Lord, till he should plead our cause. When we arrived at New-France we were forbidden praying one with another, or joining together in the service of God.

The next day, soon after we marched, we had an alarm; on which many of the English were bound. I was then near the front, and my masters not with me; so I was not bound. This alarm was occasioned by some Indians shooting at geese that flew over them,

that

that put them into a considerable consternation and fright; but after they came to understand they were not pursued by the English,
they boasted, that the English would not come
out after them, as they had boasted before
we began our journey in the morning. They
killed this day two women, who were so faint
they could not travel.

The next day, in the morning, before we
travelled, one Mary Brooks, a pious young
woman, came to the wigwam where I was,
and told me, she desired to bless God, who
had inclined the heart of her master to let her
come to take her farewell of me. Said she,
by my falls on the ice yesterday I injured
myself, causing a miscarriage this night, so
that I am not able to travel far; I know they
will kill me to-day; but (says she) God has
(praised be his name) by his spirit with his
word, strengthened me to my last encounter
with death: And mentioned to me some places
of Scripture seasonably sent in for her support. And (says she) I am not afraid of death;

I

I can, through the grace of God, chearfully submit to the will of God. Pray for me (said she) at parting, that God would take me to himself. Accordingly she was killed that day. I mention it to the end, I may stir up all in their young days, to improve the death of Christ by faith, to a giving them an holy boldness in the day of death.

The next day we were made to scatter one from another into smaller companies; and one of my children carried away with Indians belonging to the eastern parts. At night my master came to me, with my pistol in his hand, and put it to my breast, and said, now I will kill you, for (said be) at your house you would have killed me with it if you could. But, by the grace of God, I was not much daunted; and whatever his intention might be, God prevented my death.

The next day I was again permitted to pray with that company of captives with me, and we allowed to sing a psalm together. After which, I was taken from all the company

of

of the English, excepting two children of my neighbours, one of which, a girl of four years of age, was killed by her Macqua master, the next morning, the snow being so deep, when we left the river, that he could not carry the child and his pack too.

When the Sabbath came, one Indian staid with me, and a little boy nine years old, whilst the rest went a hunting. And when I was here, I thought with myself, that God had now separated me from the congregation of his people, who were now in his sanctuary, where he commandeth the blessing, even life forever; and made to bewail my unfruitfulness under, and unthankfulness for such a mercy. When my spirit was almost overwhelmed within me, at the consideration of what had passed over me, and what was to be expected, I was ready almost to sink in my spirit. But God spake those words with a greater efficacy than man could speak them, for my strengthening and support: Psal. cxviii. 17. *I shall not die, but live: And declare the works*

works of the Lord. Psalm xlii. 11. *Why art thou cast down, O my soul? And why art thou disquieted within me? Hope thou in God; for I shall yet praise him, who is the health of my countenance, and my God.* Nehem. i. 8, 9. *Remember, I beseech thee, the word that thou commandest thy servant Moses, saying, if ye transgress, I will scatter you abroad among the nations: But if ye turn unto me, and keep my commandments, and do them; though there were of you cast out unto the uttermost part of the heaven, yet will I gather them from thence, and will bring them unto the place that I have chosen, to set my name there.* These three places of Scripture, one after another, by the grace of God, strengthened my hopes, that God would to far restrain the wrath of the adversary, that the greatest number of us left alive, should be carried through so tedious a journey: That though my children had no father to take care of them, that word quieted me to a patient waiting to see the end the Lord would make, Jer. xlix. 11. *Leave thy fatherless*

*fatherless children, I will preserve them alive,
and let thy widows trust in me.* Accordingly
God carried them wonderfully through great
difficulties and dangers. My youngest daughter, aged seven years, was carried all the
journey, and looked after with a great deal of
tenderness. My youngest son, aged four
years, was wonderfully preserved from death;
for though they that carried him, or drawed
him on sleighs, were tired with their journey,
yet their savage cruel tempers were so over-
ruled by God, that they did not kill him; but
in their pity, he was spared, and others would
take care of him; so that four times on the
journey he was thus preserved, till at last he
arrived at Montreal, where a French gentlewoman, pitying the child, redeemed it out
of the hands of the heathen. My son Samuel, and my eldest daughter, were pitied, so
as to be drawn on sleighs, when unable to
travel. And though they suffered very much
through scarcity of food, and tedious journeys, they were carried through to Montreal.
                                          And

And my son Stephen, about eleven years of
age, wonderfully preserved from death, in the
famine whereof three English persons died,
and after eight months brought into Chamblee.
My master returned on the evening of the
Sabbath, and told me, he had killed five
moose. The next day we removed to the
place where he had killed them. We tarried
there three days, till we had roasted and dried
the meat. My master made me a pair of
snow-shoes, for (said he) you cannot pos-
sibly travel without, the snow being knee-
deep. We parted from thence heavy laden;
I travelled with a burden on my back, with
snow-shoes, twenty-five miles the first day of
wearing them; and again the next day till
afternoon; and then we came to the French
river. My master, at this place, took away
my pack, and drawed the whole load on the
ice; but my bones seemed to be misplaced,
and I unable to travel with any speed. My
feet were very sore, and each night I wrung
blood out of my stockings, when I pulled them
off.

off. My shins also were very sore, being cut with crusty snow, in the time of my travelling without snow-shoes. But finding some dry oak-leaves, by the river banks, I put them to my shins; and in once applying of them, they were healed. And here my master was very kind to me, would always give me the best he had to eat; and by the goodness of God, I never wanted a meal's meat, during my captivity; though some of my children and neighbours were greatly wounded, (as I may say) with the arrows of famine and pinching want; having for many days nothing but roots to live upon, and not much of them neither. My master gave me a piece of a Bible; never disturbing me in reading the Scriptures, or in praying to God. Many of my neighbours, also, found that mercy in their journey, to have Bibles, psalm books, catechisms, and good books, put into their hands, with liberty to use them; and yet after their arrival at Canada, all possible endeavours were used to deprive them of them. Some of

them

them say, their Bibles were demanded by the French priests, and never re-delivered to them, to their great grief and sorrow.

My march on the French river was very sore; for fearing a thaw, we travelled a very great pace; my feet were so bruised, and my joints so distorted by my travelling in snow shoes, that I thought it impossible to hold out. One morning, a little before break of day, my master came and awakened me out of my sleep, saying, arise, pray to God, and eat your breakfast, for we must go a great way to-day. After prayer, I arose from my knees, but my feet were so tender, swoln, bruised, and full of pain, that I could scarce stand upon them, without holding on the wigwam. And when the Indians said, you must run to-day; I answered, I could not run: My master pointing out to his hatchet, said to me, then I must dash out your brains, and take off your scalp. I said, I suppose then you will do so, for I am not able to travel with speed. He sent me away alone on the ice. About sun

sun half an hour high, he over-took me, for
I had gone very slowly, not thinking it possible to travel five miles. When he came up,
he called me to run; I told him I could go no
faster. He passed by without saying one
word more; so that sometimes I scarce saw
any thing of him for an hour together. I
travelled from about break of day till dark;
never so much as set down at noon to eat
warm victuals; eating frozen meat, which I
had in my coat pocket, as I travelled. We
went that day two of their day's journey, as
they came down. I judge we went forty or
forty-five miles that day. God wonderfully
supported me; and so far renewed my strength,
that in the afternoon I was stronger to travel
than in the forenoon. My strength was re-
stored and renewed to admiration. We should
never distrust the care and compassion of
God, who can give strength to them who
have no might, and power to them who are
ready to faint.

When we entered on the lake, the ice was
very

very rough and uneven, which was very griev-
ous to my feet, that could scarce endure to
be set down on the smooth ice, on the river.
I lifted up my cry to God in ejaculatory requests, that he would take notice of my state,
and some way or other relieve me. I had not
marched above half a mile, before there fell
a moist snow, about an inch and half deep,
that made it very soft for my feet, to pass
over the lake, to the place where my master's
family was. Wonderful favours in the midst
of trying afflictions! We went a day's journey from the lake, to a small company of Indians, who were a hunting; they were, after
their manner, kind to me, and gave me the
best they had, which was moose flesh, ground-
nuts, and cramberries, but no bread. For three
weeks together I eat no bread. After our
stay there, and undergoing difficulties in cutting of wood, and suffering from lousiness,
having lousy old clothes of soldiers put upon
me, when they stript me of mine, to sell to
the French soldiers in the army.

We

We again began a march for Chamblee; we stayed at a branch of the lake, and feasted two or three days on geese we killed there. After another day's travel, we came to a river where the ice was thawed; we made a canoe of elm-bark in one day, and arrived on a Saturday near noon, at Chamblee, a small village, where is a garrison and fort of French soldiers.

[*At* CHAMBLEE.]

This village is about fifteen miles from Montreal. The French were very kind to me. A gentleman of the place took me into his house, and to his table; and lodged me at night on a good feather-bed. The inhabitants and officers were very obliging to me, the little time I staid with them, and promised to write a letter to the governour in chief, to inform him of my passing down the river. Here I saw a girl taken from our town, and a young man, who informed me, that the greatest part of the captives were come in, and that two of my children were at Montreal; that
many

many of the captives had been in three weeks before my arrival. Mercy in the midst of judgment! As we passed along the river towards Sorel, we went into a house, where was an English woman of our town, who had been left among the French in order to her conveyance to the Indian fort. The French were very kind to her, and to myself, and gave us the best provision they had; and she embarked with us, to go down to St. François fort. When we came down to the first inhabited house at Sorel, a French woman came to the river side, and desired us to go into her house; and when we were entered, she compassioned our state, and told us, she had in the last war been a captive among the Indians, and therefore was not a little sensible of our difficulties. She gave the Indians something to eat in the chimney corner, and spread a cloth on the table for us with napkins; which gave such offence to the Indians, that they hasted away, and would not call in at the fort. But wherever we entered into houses, the
French

French were very courteous. When we came
to St. François river, we found some difficulty
by reason of the ice; and entering a Frenchman's house, he gave us a loaf of bread, and
some fish to carry away with us; but we passed
down the river till night, and there seven of
us supped on the fish called bull-head or
pout, and did not eat it up, the fish was so
very large.

The next morning we met with such a
great quantity of ice, that we were forced to
leave our canoe, and travel on land. We
went to a French officer's house, who took us
into a private room, out of the sight of the
Indians, and treated us very courteously.
That night we arrived at the fort called St.
François; where we found several poor children, who had been taken from the eastward
the summer before; a sight very affecting,
they being in habit very much like Indians,
and in manners very much symbolizing with
them. At this fort lived two Jesuits, one of
which was made superiour of the Jesuits of
Quebec.

Quebec. One of these Jesuits met me at the
fort gate, and asked me to go into the church
and give God thanks for preserving my life.
I told him I would do that in some other
place. When the bell rang for evening prayers, he that took me, bid me go; but I refused.
The Jesuit came to our wigwam, and prayed
a short prayer, and invited me to sup with
them, and justified the Indians in what they
did against us; rehearsing some things done
by Major Walden, above thirty years ago;
and how justly God retaliated them in the
last war, and inveighed against us for beginning this war with the Indians: And said, we
had before the last winter, and in the
winter, been very barbarous and cruel, in
burning and killing Indians. I told them,
that the Indians, in a very perfidious manner,
had committed murders on many of our inhabitants, after the signing articles of peace:
And as to what they spake of cruelties, they
were undoubtedly falsehoods, for I well
knew the English were not approvers of an
                                    inhumanity

inhumanity or barbarity towards enemies. They said, an Englishman had killed one of St. Casteen's relations, which occasioned this war; for, say they, the nations, in a general counsel, had concluded not to engage in the war, on any side, till they themselves were first molested, and then all of them, as one, would engage against them that began a war with them; and that upon the killing of Casteen's kinsman, a post was dispatched to Canada, to advertise the Macquas, and Indians, that the English had begun a war: On which they gathered up their forces, and that the French joined with them, to come down on the eastern parts; and that when they came near New-England, several of the eastern Indians told them of the peace made with the English, and the satisfaction given them from the English for that murder. But the Macquas told them, it was now too late; for they were sent for, and were now come, and would fall on them, if without their consent they made a peace with the English. Said also, that a

letter

letter was shown them, sent from the governour of Port-Royal, which, he said, was taken
in an English ship, being a letter from the
queen of England to our governour, writing
how she approved his designs to ensnare and
deceitfully to seize on the Indians; so that
being enraged from that letter, and being
forced, as it were, they began the present
war. I told them the letter was a lie, forged
by the French.

The next morning the bell rang for mass:
My master bid me go to church: I refused:
He threatened me, and went away in a rage.
At noon, the Jesuits sent for me to dine with
them; for I eat at their table all the time I
was at the fort. And after dinner, they told
me, the Indians would not allow of any of
their captives staying in their wigwams, whilst
they were at church; and were resolved by
force and violence to bring us all to church,
if we would not go without. I told them it
was highly unreasonable so to impose upon
those who were of a contrary religion; and to
force

force us to be present at such service, as we
abhorred, was nothing becoming Christianity.
They replied, they were savages, and would
not hearken to reason, but would have their
wills; Said also, if they were in New-England
themselves, they would go into their churches,
to see their ways of worship. I answered,
the case was far different, for there was nothing (themselves being judges) as to matter
or manner of worship, but what was according to the word of God, in our churches; and
therefore it could not be an offence to any
man's conscience. But among them, there
were idolatrous superstitions in worship. They
said, Come and see, and offer us conviction
of what is superstitious in worship. To
which I answered, That I was not to do evil
that good might come on it; and that forcing
in matters of religion was hateful. They answered, The Indians were resolved to have
it so, and they could not pacify them without
my coming; and they would engage they
should offer no force or violence to cause any
compliance with their ceremonies.   The

The next mass, my master bid me go to
church: I objected; he arose, and forcibly
pulled me by my head and shoulders out of
the wigwam to the church, which was near
the door. So I went in, and sat down behind
the door; and there saw a great confusion,
instead of any gospel order; for one of the
Jesuits was at the altar, saying mass in a
tongue unknown to the savages; and the other,
between the altar and the door, saying and
singing prayers among the Indians at the
same time; and many others were at the same
time saying over their pater nosters, and Ave
Mary, by tale from their chapelit, or beads on
a string. At our going out, we smiled at
their devotion so managed; which was offen-
sive to them; for they said we made a derision
of their worship. When I was here, a certain savagess died; one of the Jesuits told me
she was a very holy woman, who had not
committed one sin in twelve years. After a
day or two, the Jesuits asked me what I
thought of their way, now I saw it? I told
                                          them,

them, I thought Christ said of it, as Mark vii. 7, 8, 9. *Howbeit, in vain do they worship me, teaching for doctrines the commandments of men. For laying aside the commandment of God, ye hold the tradition of men, as the washing of pots and cups; and many other such like things ye do. And he said unto them, Full well ye reject the commandment of God, that ye may keep your own tradition.* They told me, they were not the commandments of men but apostolical traditions, of equal authority with the holy Scriptures: And that after my death, I should bewail my not praying to the Virgin Mary; and that I should find the want of her intercession for me with her son; judging me to hell for asserting the Scriptures to be a perfect rule of faith: And said, I abounded in my own sense, entertaining explications contrary to the sense of the pope, regularly sitting with a general council, explaining Scripture, and making articles of faith. I told them, it was my comfort that Christ was to be my judge, and not they,

at

at the great day; and as for their censuring
and judging me, I was not moved with it.

One day, a certain savagess, taken prisoner
in Philip's war, who had lived at Mr. Buck-
ley's at Weathersfield, called Ruth, who could
speak English very well, who had been often
at my house, but was now proselyted to the
Romish faith, came into the wigwam, and
with her an English maid, who was taken the
last war, who was dressed up in Indian ap-
parel, unable to speak one word of English,
who said she could neither tell her own name,
or the name of the place from whence she
was taken. These two talked in the Indian
dialect with my master a long time; after
which, my master bade me cross myself; I
told him I would not; he commanded me several times, and I as often refused. Ruth
said, Mr. Williams, you know the Scripture,
and therfore act against your own light; for
you know the Scripture saith, *servants obey
your masters:* he is your master, and you his
servant. I told her she was ignorant, and
                                              knew

knew not the meaning of the Scriptures, telling her, I was not to disobey the great God to obey any master, and that I was ready to suffer for God, if called thereto: On which she talked to my master; I suppose she interpreted what I said. My master took hold of my hand to force me to cross myself; but I struggled with him, and would not suffer him to guide my hand; upon this, he pulled off a crucifix from his own neck, and bade me kiss it; but I refused once and again; he told me he would dash out my brains with his hatchet if I refused. I told him I should sooner choose death than to sin against God. Then he ran and catched up his hatchet, and acted as though he would have dashed out my brains. Seeing I was not moved, he threw down his hatchet, saying he would first bite off all my nails if I still refused. I gave him my hand, and told him I was ready to suffer; he set his teeth in my thumb nail, and gave a gripe with his teeth, and then said, *no good minister, no love God, as bad as the devil;* and

so

so left off. I have reason to bless God, who
strengthened me to withstand. By this he
was so discouraged as never more to meddle
with me about my religion. I asked leave
of the Jesuits to pray with those English of our
town who were with me; but they absolutely
refused to give us any permission to pray one
with another, and did what they could to
prevent our having any discourse together.

After a few days, the Governour de Vaudreuil, governour in chief, sent down two men
with letters to the Jesuits, desiring them to
order my being sent up to him to Montreal;
upon which, one of the Jesuits went with my
two masters, and took me along with them,
as also two more of Deerfield, a man, and his
daughter about seven years of age. When we
came to the lake, the wind was tempestuous,
and contrary to us, so that they were afraid to
go over; they landed, and kindled a fire, and
said they would wait a while to see whether
the wind would fall or change. I went aside
from the company, among the trees, and
                                    spread

spread our case, with the temptations of it, before God, and pleaded that he would order the season so, that we might not go back again, but be furthered on our voyage, that I might have opportunity to see my children and neighbours, and converse with them, and know their state.   When I returned, the wind was more boisterous; and then a second time, and the wind was more fierce. I reflected upon myself for my unquietness, and the want of a resigned will to the will of God.   And a third time went and bewailed before God my anxious cares, and the tumultuous workings of my own heart, begged a will fully resigned to the will of God, and thought that by the grace of God I was brought to say *amen* to whatever God should determine.   Upon my return to the company, the wind was yet high: The Jesuit and my master said, Come, we will go back again to the fort, for there is no likelihood of proceeding in our voyage, for very frequently such a wind continues three days, sometimes six.   After it continued so

many

many hours, I said to them, The will of the Lord be done; and the canoe was put again into the river, and we embarked. No sooner had my master put me into the canoe, and put off from the shore, but the wind fell; and coming into the middle of the river, they said, We may go over the lake well enough: And so we did. I promised if God gave me opportunity, I would stir up others to glorify God in a continued persevering, committing their straits of heart to him. He is a prayer-hearing God, and the stormy winds obey him. After we passed over the lake, the French, wherever we came, were very compassionate to us.

[*At* M O N T R E A L.]

When I came to Montreal, which was eight weeks after my captivity, the Governour de Vaudreuil redeemed me out of the hands of the Indians, gave me good clothing, took me to his table, gave me the use of a very good chamber, and was in all respects, relating to my outward man, courteous and charitable

to

to admiration. At my first entering into his house, he sent for my two children, who were in the city, that I might see them; and promised to do what he could to get all my children and neighbours out of the hands of the savages. My change of diet, after the difficulties of my journeys, caused an alteration in my body: I was physicked, blooded, and very tenderly taken care of in my sickness. The governour redeemed my eldest daughter out of the hands of the Indians; and she was carefully tended in the hospital, until she was well of her lameness; and by the governour provided for with respect, during her stay in the country. My youngest child was redeemed by a gentlewoman in the city, as the Indians passed by. After the Indians had been at their fort, and discoursed with the priests, they came back, and offered to the gentlewoman a man for the child, alleging that the child could not be profitable to her, but the man would, for he was a weaver, and his service would much advance the design she had of making cloth:

But

But God over-ruled so far, that this temptation to the woman prevailed not for an exchange; for had the child gone to the Indian
fort, in an ordinary way it had abode there
still, as the rest of the children carried thither
do. The governour gave orders to certain
officers to get the rest of my children out of
the hands of the Indians, and as many of my
neighbours as they could. After six weeks, a
merchant of the city obtained my eldest son,
who was taken to live with him. He took a
great deal of pains to persuade the savages
to part with him. An Indian came to the
city (Sagamore George of Pennicook) from
Cowass, and brought word of my son Stephen's being near Cowass, and some money
was put into his hand for his redemption, and
a promise of full satisfaction if he brought
him; but the Indian proved unfaithful, and I
never saw my child till a year after.

The governour ordered a priest to go
along with me to see my youngest daughter
among the Macquas, and endeavour for her
                                    ransom

ransom. I went with him; he was very courteous to me; and from his parish, which was
near the Macqua fort, he wrote a letter to the
Jesuit, to desire him to send my child to see
me, and to speak with them who took her,
to come along with her. But the Jesuit wrote
back a letter, That I should not be permitted
to speak with, or see my child; and if I came,
my labour would be lost; and that the Macquas would as soon part with their hearts as
my child. At my return to the city, I with an
heavy heart carried the Jesuit's letter to the
governour, who, when he read it, was very
angry, and endeavoured to comfort me, assuring me I should see her, and speak with
her; and he would to his utmost endeavour for
her ransom. Accordingly, he sent to the Jesuits, who were in the city, and bid them improve their interest for the obtaining the
child. After some days, he went with me in
his own person to the fort. When we came
thither, he discoursed with the Jesuits; after
which, my child was brought into the chamber
where

where I was. I was told I might speak
with her, but should be permitted to speak to
no other English person there. My child was
about seven years old; I discoursed with her
near an hour; she could read very well, and
had not forgotten her catechism; and was very
desirous to be redeemed out of the hands of
the Macquas, and bemoaned her state among
them, telling me how they profaned God's
Sabbaths; and said, She thought that a few
days before they had been mocking the devil,
and that one of the Jesuits stood and looked
on them. I told her, she must pray to God
for his grace every day. She said, she did
as she was able, and God helped her; but,
says she, They force me to say some prayers
in Latin, but I do not understand one word of
them; I hope it will not do me any harm. I
told her, she must be careful she did not forget her catechism, and the Scriptures she had
learnt by heart. She told the captives after
I was gone, as some of them have since informed me, almost every thing I spake to her;
and

and said, she was much afraid she should forget her catechism, having none to instruct
her. I saw her once, a few days after, in the
city, but had not many minutes of time with
her; but what time I had, I improved to give
her the best advice I could. The governour
laboured much for her redemption; at last he
had a promise of it, in case he would procure
for them an Indian girl in her stead. Accordingly, he sent up the river, some hundreds
of leagues, for one; but it was refused, when
offered by the governour. He offered them
an hundred pieces of eight for her redemption, but it was refused. His lady went over
to beg her from them, but all in vain; she is
there still; and has forgotten to speak English.
Oh! that all who peruse this history would
join in their fervent requests to God, with
whom all things are possible, that this poor
child, and so many others of our children
who have been cast upon God from the
womb, and are now outcasts ready to perish,
might be gathered from their dispersions,
and receive sanctifying grace from God!

When

When I had discoursed with the child, and was coming out of the fort, one of the Jesuits went out of the chamber with me, and some soldiers, to convey me to the canoe. I saw some of my poor neighbours, who stood with longing expectations to see me, and speak with me, and had leave from their savage masters so to do. I was by the Jesuit himself thrust along by force, and permitted only to tell them some of their relations (they asked after) were well in the city, and that with a very audible voice; being not permitted to come near to them. After my return to the city I was very melancholy, for I could not be permitted so much as to pray with the English, who dwelt in the same house. And the English, who came to see me, were most of them put back by the guard at the door, and not suffered to come and speak with me. Sometimes the guard was so strict that I could scarce go aside on necessary occasions without a repulse; and whenever I went out into the city (a favour the governour himself
never

never refused when I asked it of him) there were spies to watch me, and to observe whether I spake to the English. Upon which I told some of the English, they must be careful to call to mind and improve former instructions, and endeavour to stand at a further distance for a while, hoping that after a short time I should have more liberty of conversing with them. But some spies, sent out, found on a Sabbath day more than three (the number we, by their order published, were not to exeed together) of us in company, who informed the priest; the next day one of the priests told me, I had a greater number of the English with me, and that I had spoken something reflecting on their religion. I spake to the governour, desiring that no forcible means might be used with any of the captives respecting their religion; he told me, he allowed no such thing. I am persuaded that the governour, if he might act himself, would not have suffered such things to be done as have been done, and that

he

he never did know of several things acted against the English.

At my first coming to Montreal, the governour told me, I should be sent home as soon as Captain Battiss was returned, and not before; and that I was taken in order to his redemption. The governour sought by all means to divert me from my melancholy sorrows, and always shewed a willingness for seeing my children. And one day I told him of my design of walking into the city; he pleasantly answered, Go with all my heart. His eldest son went with me as far as the door and saw the guard stop me; he went in and informed his father, who came to the door and asked, why they affronted the gentleman going out? They said, it was their order: But with an angry countenance he said, his orders were that I should not be stopt. But within a little time I had my orders to go down to Quebec. Another thing shewing that many things are done without the governour's consent, though his name be used to justify them,

them, (viz.) I asked the priest, after I had
been at Montreal two days, leave to go and
see my youngest child; he said, Whenever
you would see him, tell me, and I will bring
him to you; for, says he, the governour is not
willing you should go thither. / And yet, not
many days after, when we were at dinner,
the governour's lady (seeing me sad) spake
to an officer at table, who could speak Latin,
to tell me, that after dinner I should go along
with them and see my two children. And
accordingly after dinner I was carried to see
them; and when I came to the house, I found
three or four English captives, who lived
there, and I had leave to discourse with them.
And not long after, the governour's lady asked
me to go along with her to the hospital, to
see one of my neighbours sick there.

One day one of the Jesuits came to the governour, and told the company there, that he
never saw such persons as were taken from
Deerfield. Said he, The Macquas will not
suffer any of their prisoners to abide in their
wigwams

wigwams whilst they themselves are at mass,
but carry them with them to the church, and
they cannot be prevailed with to fall down on
their knees to pray there; but no sooner are
they returned to their wigwams, but they fall
down on their knees to prayer. He said,
they could do nothing with the grown persons
there; and they hindered the children's com-
plying. Whereupon, the Jesuits counselled
the Macquas to sell all the grown persons
from the fort; a stratagem to seduce poor
children. Oh Lord! Turn the counsels of
these Ahitophels into foolishness, and make
the counsels of the heathen of none effect!

Here I observed, they were wonderfully
lifted up with pride, after the return of Captain Montigny from Northampton, with news
of success: They boasted of their success
against New-England. And they sent out
an army, as they said, of seven hundred men,
if I mistake not, two hundred of whom were
French, in company of which army went
several Jesuits; and said, they would lay desolate

late all the places on Connecticut river. The
superiour of the priests told me, their general was a very prudent and brave commander
of undaunted courage, and doubted not but
they should have great success. This army
went away in such a boasting, triumphant
manner, that I had great hopes God would
discover and disappoint their designs; our
prayers were not wanting for the blasting
such a bloody design. The superiour of the
priests said to me, Do not flatter yourselves
in hopes of a short captivity; for, said he,
there are two young princes contending for
the kingdom of Spain; and a third, that care
was to be taken for his establishment on the
English throne. And boasted what they would
do in Europe; and that we must expect not
only in Europe, but in New-England, the establishment of popery. I said, Glory not,
God can make great changes in a little time,
and revive his own interest, and yet save his
poor afflicted people. Said he, The time for
miracles is past; and in the time of the last
                                                        war,

war, the king of France was, as it were, against all the world, and yet did very great things; but now the kingdom of Spain is for him, and the duke of Bavaria, and the duke of Savoy, &c. and spake in a lofty manner of great things to be done by them; and having the world, as I may say, in subjection to them.

I was sent down to Quebec in company of Governour de Ramsey, governour of Montreal, and the superiour of the Jesuits, and ordered to live with one of the council; from whom I received many favours for seven weeks. He told me, it was the priests' doings to send me down before the governour came down; and that if I went much to see the English, or they came much to visit me, I should yet certainly be sent away, where I should have no converse with the English.

[*At* QUEBEC.]

After my coming down to Quebec, I was invited to dine with the Jesuits, and to my face they were civil enough. But after a few days, a young gentleman came to my chamber,

ber, and told me, that one of the Jesuits (after we had done dinner) made a few distichs of verses, and gave them to his scholars to translate into French: He shewed them to me. The import of them was, "That the "king of France's grand-son had sent out his "huntsmen, and that they had taken a wolf, "who was shut up, and now he hopes the sheep "would be in safety." I knew, at the reading of them, what he aimed at; but held my peace, as though I had been ignorant of the Jesuit's intention. Observing this reproaching spirit, I said in my heart, If God will bless, let men curse if they please: And I looked to God in Christ, the great shepherd, to keep his scattered sheep among so many Romish ravenous wolves, and to remember the reproaches wherewith his holy name, ordinances, and servants were daily reproached. And upon an observation of the time of these verses being composed, I find that near the same time the bishop of Canada, with twenty ecclesiasticks, were taken by the English, as they
were

were coming from France, and carried into England as prisoners of war.

One Sabbath day morning, I observed many signs of approaching rain, a great moisture on the stones of the hearth and chimney jambs. I was that day invited to dine with the Jesuits; and when I went up to dinner it began to rain a small drizzling rain: The superiour told me, they had been praying for rain that morning: And lo, (says he), it begins to rain. I told him, I could tell him of many instances of God's hearing our prayers for rain. However, in the afternoon there was a general procession of all orders, priests, Jesuits and friars, and the citizens, in great pomp, carrying (as they said) as an holy relick, one of the bones of St. Paul. The next day I was invited to the priests' seminary to dinner; Oh, said they, we went in procession yesterday for rain, and see what a plentiful rain followed. I answered, We had been answered when praying for rain, when no such signs of rain, and the beginnings of rain preceded,

preceded, as now with them, before they appointed or began their procession, &c. However, they upbraided me, that God did not approve of our religion, in that he disregarded our prayers, and accepted theirs. For (said they) we heard you had days of fasting and prayer before the fleet came to Quebec; God would not regard your prayers, but heard ours, and almost in a miraculous way preserved us when assaulted, and refused to hear your fast-day prayers for your preservation, but heard ours for your desolation, and our success. They boasted also of their king, and his greatness, and spake of him as though there could be no settlement in the world but as he pleased; reviling us as in a low and languishing case, having no king, but being under the government of a queen: And spake as though the duke of Bavaria would in a short time be emperour. From this day forward God gave them to hear sorrowful tidings from Europe: That a war was commenced against the duke of Savoy, and so their enemies increased:

increased: Their bishop taken, and two millions of wealth with him. News every year
more distressing and impoverishing to them;
and the duke of Bavaria, so far from being
emperour, that he is dispossessed of his duke-
dom; and France, so far from being strengthened by Spain, that the kingdom of Spain
was like to be an occasion of the weakening
and impoverishing their own kingdom; they
themselves so reporting. And their great
army going against New-England turned back
ashamed; and they discouraged and disheartened; and every year, very exercising
fears and cares, as to the savages who live
up the river. Before the return of that army,
they told me, We were led up and down, and
sold by the heathen, as sheep for the slaughter,
and they could not devise what they should do
with us, we should be so many prisoners, when
the army returned. The Jesuits told me, it
was a great mercy that so many of our children were brought to them, and that now, especially since they were not like speedily to
be

be returned, there was hope of their being
brought over to the Romish faith. They
would take the English children, born among
them, and against the consent of their parents,
baptize them. One Jesuit came to me and
asked, whether all the English at Loret, (a
place not far from Quebec, where the savages
lived), were baptized ? I told him they were.
He said, If they be not, let me know of it, that
I may baptize them, for fear they should die
and be damned, if they died without baptism. Says he, When the savages went against
you, I charged them to baptize all children
before they killed them; such was my desire
of your eternal salvation, though you were our
enemies. There was a gentleman called Monsieur de Beauville, a captain, the brother of
the lord intendant, who was a good friend to
me, and very courteous to all the captives; he
lent me an English Bible, and when he went
to France, gave it me.

All means were used to seduce poor souls.

I was invited one day to dine with one of
                                    chief

chief note; as I was going, I met with the
superiour of the Jesuits coming out of the
house, and he came in after dinner; and presently it was propounded to me, if I would
stay among them, and be of their religion, I
should have a great and honourable pension
from the king every year. The superiour of
the Jesuits turned to me, and said, "Sir, you
'have manifested much grief and sorrow for
'your separation from so many of your neigh-
'bours and children; if you will now comply
'with this offer and proposal, you may have
'all your children with you; and here will be
'enough for an honourable maintenance for
'you and them." I answered, Sir, if I thought
your religion to be true, I would embrace it
freely without any such offer; but so long as I
believe it to be what it is, the offer of the whole
world is of no more value to me than a black-
berry; and manifested such an abhorrence of
this proposal, that I speedily went to take my
leave and be gone. Oh! Sir, (said he) sit down.
Why in such a hurry? You are alone in
your

your chamber, divert yourself a little longer;
and fell to other discourse; and within half
an hour says again, Sir, I have one thing earnestly to request of you, I pray pleasure me!
I said, Let your lordship speak; said he, I
pray come down to the palace to-morrow
morning, and honour me with your company
in my coach to the great church, it being then
a saint's day. I answered, Ask me any thing
wherein I can serve you with a good conscience, and I am ready to gratify you, but I
must ask your excuse here; and immediately
went away from him. Returning unto my
chamber, I gave God thanks for his uphold-
ing of me; and also made an inquiry with
myself, whether I had, by any action, given
encouragement for such a temptation.

[*At* C H A T E A U V I C H E .]

Not many days after, and a few days before Governour de Vaudreuil's coming down,
I was sent away, fifteen miles down the river,
that I might not have opportunity of converse
with the English. I was courteously treated
by

by the French, and the priest of that parish; they told me he was one of the most learned men in the country; he was a very ingenious man, zealous in their way, but yet very familiar. I had many disputes with the priests who came thither; and when I used their own authors to confute some of their positions, my books, borrowed of them, were taken away from me, for they said, I made an ill use of them. They having, many of them, boasted of their unity in doctrine and profession, were loth I should show them, from their own best approved authors, as many different opinions as they could charge against us. Here, again, a gentleman, in the presence of the old bishop and a priest, offered me his house, and whole living, with assurance of honour, wealth and employment, if I would embrace their ways. I told them, I had an indignation of soul against such offers on such terms, as parting with what was more valuable than all the world; alleging, *What is a man profited if he gain the whole world, and lose his own soul?*

or

or what shall a man give in exchange for his soul? I was sometimes told, I might have all my children if I would comply, and must never expect to have them on any other terms. I told them, my children were dearer to me than all the world, but I would not deny Christ and his truths for the having of them with me; I would still put my trust in God, who could perform all things for me.

I am persuaded that the priest of that parish, where I kept, abhorred their sending down the heathen to commit outrages against the English, saying, it was more like committing murders, than managing a war. In my confinement in this parish, I had my undisturbed opportunities to be humbly imploring grace for ourselves, for soul and body, for his protecting presence with New-England, and his disappointing the bloody designs of enemies; that God would be a little sanctuary to us in a land of captivity, and that our friends in New-England might have grace to make a more thankful and fruitful improve-
ment

ment of the means of grace than we had done; who, by our neglects, find ourselves out of God's sanctuary.

On the twenty-first of October, 1704, I received some letters from New-England, with an account that many of our neighbours escaped out of the desolations in the fort, and that my dear wife was carried back, and decently buried: And that my eldest son, who was absent in our desolation, was sent to college, and provided for; which occasioned thanksgiving to God in the midst of afflictions, and caused prayers, even in Canada, to be going daily up to Heaven for a blessing upon benefactors, showing such kindness to the desolate and afflicted. The consideration of such crafty designs to ensnare young ones, and to turn them from the simplicity of the gospel to Romish superstition, was very exercising; sometimes they would tell me my children, sometimes my neighbours, were turned to be of their religion. Some made it their work to allure poor souls by flatteries and great promises,

promises, some threatened, some offered abusive carriage to such as refused to go to church and be present at mass. Some they industriously contrived to get married among them. A priest drew up a compendium of the Roman Catholick faith, and pretended to prove it by the Scriptures, telling the English, that all they required was contained in the Scriptures, which they acknowledged to be the rule of faith and manners; but it was by Scriptures horribly perverted and abused. I could never come to the sight of it, (though I often earnestly entreated a copy of it), until I was on shipboard, for our voyage to New-England; but hearing of it, I endeavoured to possess the English with their danger of being cheated with such a pretence. I understood they would tell the English that I was turned, that they might gain them to change their religion. These their endeavours to seduce to popery were very exercising to me: And in my solitariness I drew up these following sorrowful, mournful considerations, though unused

unused to, and unskilful in poetry, yet in a plain style, for use of some of the captives, who would sometimes make their secret visits to me, which, at the desire of some of them, are here made publick.

Some contemplations of the poor and desolate state of the church at Deerfield.

THE sorrows of my heart enlarged are,
Whilst I my present state with past compare.
I frequently unto God's house did go,
With Christian friends, his praises forth to
    show.
But now, I solitary sit, both sigh and cry,
Whilst my flock's misery think on do I.
    Many, both old & young, were slain out-
        right;
Some, in a bitter season, took their flight.
Some burnt to death, and others stifled were;
The enemy no sex or age would spare.
The tender children, with their parents sad,
Are carried forth as captives, some unclad.
                                        Some

Some murdered in the way, unburied left,
And some, through famine, were of life bereft.
After a tedious journey, some are sold,
Some kept in heathen hands, all from Christ's
    fold:
By popish rage, and heath'nish cruelty,
Are banished. Yea some compell'd to be
Present at mass. Young children parted are
From parents, and such as instructors were.
Crafty designs are us'd by papists all,
In ignorance of truth, them to inthrall.
Some threat'ned are, unless they will
    comply,
In heathen's hands again be made to lie.
To some, large promises are made, if they
Will truths renounce, & choose their popish
    way.
    Oh Lord! mine eyes on thee shall waiting be,
Till thou again turn our captivity.
Their Romish plots, thou canst confound; &
    save
This little flock, this mercy I do crave.
Save us from all our sins, and yet again
                      Deliver

Deliver us from them who truth disdain.
Lord! for thy mercy sake, thy cov'nant
    mind;
And in thy house again, rest let us find.
So we thy praises forth will shew, and speak
of all thy wond'rous works, yea we will seek
The advancement of thy great and glorious
    name,
Thy rich and sovereign grace we will proclaim.

THE hearts of some were ready to be discouraged and sink, saying, They were out of
sight, and so out of mind. I endeavoured to
persuade them we were not forgotten, that
undoubtedly many prayers were continually
going up to heaven for us. Not long after,
came Captain Livingston, and Mr. Sheldon,
with letters from his excellency our governour to the governour of Canada, about the
exchange of prisoners; which gave a revival
to many, and raised expectations of a return.
These visits from New-England to Canada,
so often, greatly strengthened many who
                                            were

were ready to faint; and gave some check
to the designs of the papists to gain proselytes. But God's time of deliverance was not
yet come; as to some particular persons, their
temptations and trials were increased; and
some abused, because they refused a
compliance with their superstitions. A young
woman of our town met with a new trial; for
on a day, a Frenchman came into the room
where she was, and shewed her his beads, and
boasted of them, putting them near to her;
she knocked them out of his hands on the
floor; for which she was beaten, and threatened with death, and for some days impris-
oned. I pleaded with God his over-ruling
this first essay for the deliverance of some, as
a pledge of the rest being delivered in due
time. I implored Captain de Beauville, who
had always been very friendly, to intercede
with the governour for the return of my eldest daughter; and for his purchasing my son
Stephen from the Indians at St. François
fort; and for liberty to go up and see my
children

children and neighbours at Montreal. Divine providence appeared to the moderating my affliction, in that five English persons of our town were permitted to return with Captain Livingston, among whom went my eldest daughter. And my son Stephen was redeemed, and sent to live with me: He was almost quite naked, and very poor; he had suffered much among the Indians. One of the Jesuits took upon him to come to the wigwam and whip him, on some complaint that the squaws had made, that he did not work enough for them. As to my petition for going up to Montreal to see my children and neighbours, it was denied; as my former desire of coming up to the city, before Captain Livingston's coming was. God granted me favour as to two of my petitions, but yet brought me by his grace to be willing, that he should glorify himself in disposing of me and mine as he pleased, and knew to be most for his glory: And almost always before any remarkable favour, I was brought to lie
down

down at the foot of God, and made to be
willing that God should govern the world
so as might be most for his own honour, and
brought to resign all to his holy sovereignty:
A frame of spirit, when wrought in me by the
grace of God, giving the greatest content and
satisfaction; and very often a fore-runner of
the mercy asked of God, or a plain demonstra-
tion, that the not obtaining my request was
best for me. I had no small refreshing, in
having one of my children with me for four
months. And the English were, many of
them, strengthened with hopes, that the
treaty betwixt the governments would issue in
opening a door of escape for all.

In August, Mr. Dudley, and Captain Vetch
arrived, and great encouragements were given
as to an exchange of all in the spring of the
year: And some few again were sent home;
among whom I obtained leave to send my son
Stephen.

Upon Mr. Dudley's and Captain Vetch's
petitioning, I was again permitted to go up
to

to Quebec; but disputing with a mendicant
friar, who said he was an Englishman sent
from France, to endeavour the conversion of
the English at Quebec, who arrived at Canada whilst our gentlemen were there, I was,
by the priests' means, ordered to return again
to Chateauviche, and no other reason given,
but because I discoursed with that priest,
and their fear I should prevent his success
amongst the captives. But God shewed his
dislike of such a persecuting spirit; for the
very next day, which was September 20, O.
S. October 1, N. S. the seminary, a very famous building, was most of it burnt down,
occasioned by a joiner's letting a coal of fire
drop among the shavings. The chapel in
the priests' garden, and the great cross, were
burnt down; the library of the priests burnt
up. This seminary and another library had
been burnt but about three years before. The
day after my being sent away, by the priests'
means, from Quebec, at first, there was a
thunder-storm, and the lightning struck the
seminary

seminary in the very place where the fire now began.

A little before Mr. Dudley's arrival, came a soldier into my landlord's house, barefoot and barelegged, going on a pilgrimage to Sainte Anne*: For, said he, my captain, who died some years ago, appeared to me, and told me he was in purgatory; and told me I must go a pilgrimage to Sainte Anne, doing penance, and get a mass said for him, and then he should be delivered. Many believed him, and were much affected with it; came and told me of it, to gain my credit of their devised purgatory. The soldier told me, the priests had counselled him to undertake this pilgrimage. And, I am apt to think, ordered his calling in at my landlord's, that I might see and speak with him. I laughed at the conceit, that a soldier must be pitched upon to be sent on this errand; but they were much displeased, and lamented my obstinacy,

in

* *Sainte Anne de Beaupré*, a village containing a famous shrine, near the *Falls of Montmorency*, 22 miles below *Quebec*.

in that I would not be reclaimed from a denial of purgatory by such a miraculous providence.

As I was able, I spread the case before God, beseeching of him to disappoint them of their expectations to proselyte any of the captives by this stratagem; and by the goodness of God, it was not very serviceable; for the soldier's conversation was such, that several among the French themselves judged it to be a forgery. And though the captain spoken of, was the governour's lady's brother, I never more heard any concernment or care to get him out of purgatory.

One of the parish, where I lived, told me, that on the twenty-second of July, 1705, he was at Quebec, at the mendicant friar's church, on one of their feast days, in honour of a great saint of their order, and that at five o'clock mass, in the morning, near two hundred persons being present, a great grey cat brake or pushed aside some glass, entered into the church, passed along near the altar, and put out five or six candles, which were
burning;

burning; and that no one could tell which
way the cat went out; and he thought it was
the devil.

When I was in the city in September, I
saw two English maids, who had lived with
the Indians a long time. They told me, that
an Indian had died at the place where they
were; and that when sundry of his relations
were together, in order to attend his burial,
the dead arose, and informed them, "That
at his death he went to hell, and there he saw
all the Indians that had been dead since their
embracing the popish religion; and warned
them to leave it off, or they would be damned
too;" and laid down dead again. They said,
the Indians were frightened, and very melancholy, but the Jesuit, to whom they told this,
told them it was only a delusion of the devil,
to draw them away from the true religion; adding, that he knew for certain that all those
Indians who had been dead, spoken of by
that Indian, were in heaven; only one squaw
was gone to hell, who died without baptism.
                                      These

These maids said also, that many of the Indians much lamented their making a war against the English, at the instigation of the French.

The priests, after Mr. Dudley's going from Canada, were ready to think their time was short for gaining English proselytes, and doubled their diligence and wiles to gain over persons to their persuasion. I improved all opportunities I could, to write to the English, that in that way I might be serviceable to them. But many or most of my letters, treating about religion, were intercepted, and burnt. I had a letter sent down to me by order of the governour, that I had liberty of writing to my children and friends, which should be continued, provided I wrote about indifferent things, and said nothing in them about the points in controversy between them and us: And if I were so hardy as to write letters otherwise, they should endeavour to prevent their being delivered. Accordingly, I found many of them were burnt. But
sometimes

sometimes notice would be given to the English, that there were letters written, but that they were burnt; so that their writing was somewhat useful, though never perused by the English, because they judged those letters condemned popery. Many of our letters, written from New-England, were never delivered, because of some expressions about religion in them. And, as I said before, after Mr. Dudley's departure from Quebec, endeavours were very vigorous to seduce. Some were flattered with large promises, others were threatened, and beaten, because they would not turn. And when two English women, who had always opposed their religion, were sick in the hospital, they kept with them night and day, till they died; and their friends kept from coming to visit them. After their death, they gave out, that they died in the Romish faith, and were received into their communion. Before their death, masses were said for them; and they were buried in the church yard, with all their ceremonies. And

And after this, letters were sent to all parts, to inform the English, that these two women turned to their religion before their death; and that it concerned them to follow their example, for they could not be more obstinate than those women were, in their health, against the Romish faith, and yet on a death bed embraced it. They told the English who lived near, that our religion was a dangerous religion to die in. But I shall hereafter relate the just grounds we have to think these things were falsehoods.

I was informed, there was an English girl bid to take and wear the cross, and cross herself: She refused; they threatened her, and shewed her the cross. At length, she had her choice, either to cross herself, and take the cross, or be whipt, she chose to be whipt; and they made as though they would correct her; but seeing her choosing indeed to suffer rather than comply, they desisted, and tied the cross about her neck. Some were taken and shut up among their religious, and all sorts of means used to gain them.   I

I received a letter from one of my neighbours, wherein he thus bewails: "I obtained
'leave of my master to go to the Macqua
'fort, to see my children, that I had not seen
'for a long time. I carried a letter from my
'master, to shew that I had leave to come.
'When I came to the fort, I heard one of my
'children was in the woods. I went to see a
'boy I had there, who lived with one of the
'Jesuits; I had just asked him of his welfare;
'he said his master would come presently;
'he durst not stay to speak with me now, be-
'ing in such awe of his master. On which, I
'withdrew; and when his master came in, I
'went and asked leave of him to speak with
'my child, and shewed him my letter. But
'he absolutely refused to let me see or speak
'with him; and said, I had brought no letter
'from the governour, and would not permit
'me to stay in the fort, though I had trav-
'elled on foot near fifty miles, for no other
'errand than to see and speak with my
'children."

The

The same person, with another Englishman, last spring, obtained leave of the governour general to go to the same fort on the
same errand, and carried letters from the
governour to the Jesuits, that he might be permitted to speak with his children. The letter
was delivered to the Jesuits; who told him,
his son was not at home, but gone a hunting:
Whereas he was hid from them, as he heard
afterward; so the poor man lost his labour a
second time. These men say, that when they
returned to Montreal, one Laland, who was
appointed as a spy, always to observe the
motions of the English, told them, that one of
the Jesuits had come in before them, and had
told the governour that the lad was gone out
a hunting: And that the Englishman, who accompanied this poor man, went out into the
woods, in hopes of finding the lad; and saw
him, but the lad run away; and that he followed him, and called after him, but he would
not stop; but holding out a gun, threatened to
shoot him down, if he followed him; and so
he

he was discouraged, and turned back. And, says Laland, you will never leave going to see your children and neighbours, till some of you are killed. But the men told him, it was an absolute lie, let who would report it; for they had neither seen the lad, nor did they go into the woods to search after him. They judge this was told to the governour, to prevent any English for the future going to see their children and neighbours. Some of ours say, they have been little better than absolutely promised to have their children, who are among the savages, in case they themselves would embrace popery. And that the priests had said, they had rather the children should be among the Indians, as they were, than be brought out by the French, and so be in readiness to return for New-England.

A maid of our town was put into a religious house, among the nuns, for more than two years, and all sorts of means, by flatteries, threatenings, and abusive carriages, used to bring her to turn. They offered her money, which

which when refused, especially the latter part of the time, they threatened her very much; sent for her before them, and commanded her to cross herself. She refused, they hit her a box on the ear; bid her again, still she refused. They ordered a rod with six branches full of knots to be brought; and when she refused, they struck her on the hands, still renewing their commands; and she stood to her refusals, till her hands were filled with wales, with the blows. But one said, Beat her no more, we will give her to the Indians, if she will not turn. They pinched her arms till they were black and blue; and made her go into their church; and because she would not cross herself, struck her several blows with their hands on her face. A squaw was brought in, and said, she was sent to fetch her to the Indians; but she refused; the squaw went away, and said, she would bring her husband with her to-morrow, and she should be carried away by force. She told me, she remembered what I told her one day, after the nuns had

threatened

threatened to give her away to the Indians; that they only said so to affright her, that they never would give her away. The nuns told her, she should not be permitted any more to speak to the English; and that they would afflict her without giving her any rest, if she refused. But God preserved her from falling. This poor girl had many prayers going up to Heaven for her daily, and by name, because her trials were more known to some of the English, than the trials of others, who lived more remote from them.

Here might be a history by itself, of the trials and sufferings of many of our children, and young ones, who have been abused, and after separation from grown persons, made to do as they would have them.

I shall here give an account of what was done to one of my children, a boy between fifteen and sixteen years of age, two hundred miles distant from me, which occasioned grief and sorrow, that I want words to utter; and yet kept under such awe, that he never

durst

durst write any thing to me, for fear of being discovered in writing about religion. They threatened to put him to the Indians again, if he would not turn; telling him, he was never bought out of their hands, but only sojourned with them, but if he would turn, he should never be put into their hands any more. The priests would spend whole days in urging him. He was sent to school to learn to read and write French; the school-master sometimes flattered him with promises, if he would cross himself; then threatened him if be would not. But when he saw flattering promises of rewards, and threatenings, were ineffectual, he struck him with a stick he had in his hand; and when he saw that would not do, he made him get down on his knees about an hour; and then came and bid him make the sign of the cross, and that without any delay; he still refused. Then he gave him a couple of strokes, with a whip he had in his hand; which whip had three branches, and about twelve great knots tied in it. And again bid him

him make the sign of the cross; and if it was
any sin, he would bear it himself: And said
also, You are afraid you shall be changed if
you do it: But (said he) you will be the same,
your fingers will not be changed. And after
he had made him shed many tears, under his
abuses and threatenings, he told him, he
would have it done: And so through cowardice and fear of the whip, he made the sign.
And did so for several days together, with
much ado, he was brought to cross himself.
And then the master told him, he would have
it done without his particular bidding him.
And when he came to say his lesson, and
crossed not himself, the master said, have
you forgot what I bid you do? No, sir, said
he; then the schoolmaster said, Down on your
knees; and so kept him for an hour and half,
till school was done; and so did for about a
week. When he saw this would not do, he
took the whip, What, will not you do it, (said
he), I will make you: And so again frighted
him to a compliance. After this, he commanded

manded him to go to the church: When he
refused, he told him, he would make him.
And one morning sent four of the biggest
boys of the school, to draw him by force to
mass. These, with other severities and witty
stratagems, were used; and I utterly ignorant
of any attempt made upon him, to bring him
to change his religion. His fear was such
that he never durst write any of these things,
lest his letters should fall into their hands, and
he should again be delivered to the Indians.
Hearing of an opportunity of writing to him
by one of the parish where I was, going up to
Montreal, I wrote a letter to him, and had by
him a letter from my son; which I shall here
insert.

"*Honoured Father,*

"I HAVE received your letter, bearing date
January 11, 1705,6; for which I give you
many thanks, with my duty and my brother's.
I am sorry you have not received all the letters I have written to you; as I have not received all yours. According to your good
counsel,

counsel, I do almost every day read something of the Bible, and so strengthen my faith. As to the captives newly brought, Lancaster is the place of two of them, and Marlborough that of the third; the governour of Montreal has them all three. There is other news that will seem more strange to you: That two English women, who in their life time were dreadfully set against the Catholick religion, did on their death bed embrace it. The one Abigail Turbet, the other of them Esther Jones, both of them known to you. Abigail Turbet sent for Mr. Meriel the Sabbath before she died; and said (many a time upon several following days) that she committed her soul into his hands, and was ready to do whatever he pleased. She desired him to go to the chapel St. Anne, and there to say a holy mass for her, that she might have her sins pardoned, and the will of the Lord accomplished upon her. Her cousin, Mrs. Badston, now Stilson, asked her, whether she should be willing to do as she said; she answered,

swered, yes. And upon the Tuesday she was
taken into the Catholick church, in the presence of John Laland, and Madam Grizalem,
an English woman, and Mrs. Stilson, also
with many French people besides. She was
anointed with oil on the same day, according
to her will then. Upon the Wednesday
following, an image of Christ crucified was
brought to her; she caused it to be set up over
against her, at the curtains of her bed, and
looked continually upon the same; and also
a little crucifix was brought unto her; she
took it, and kissed it, and laid it upon her
stomach. She did also make the sign of the
cross upon herself, when she took any meat
or drink. She promised to God, that if she
should recover, she would go to the mass every
day: She having on her hand a crucifix, said,
Oh, my Lord, that I should have known thee
so late! She did also make a prayer to the
Virgin Mary, the two last days of the week.
She could utter no word, but by kissing the
crucifix, and endeavouring to cross herself,
she

she gave an evidence of her faith. She died on Saturday the 24th of November, at three o'clock in the afternoon. The next day, the priest did commend that woman's soul to the prayers of the congregation in the mass; in the afternoon she was honourably buried in the church yard, next to the church, close to the body of the justice Pese's wife; all the people being present as her funeral. The same day, in the evening, Mr. Meriel, with an English woman, went to Esther Jones; she did at first disdain; but a little after, she confessed there were seven sacraments, Christ's body present, the sacrament of the mass, the inequality of power among the pastors of the church; and being returned to wait by her all night long, he read and expounded to her some part of the Catholick confession of faith to her satisfaction. About midnight he asked her, whether she might not confess her sins; I doubt not but I may, said she: And two hours after, she made unto him a fervent confession of all the sins of her whole life: When he

he said, he was to offer Christ to his father
for her, she liked it very well. The superiour of the nuns being come in to see her, she
now desired that she might receive Christ's
body before she died. She did also show
Mrs. Stilson a great mind to receive the sacrament of extreme unction, and said, that if
ever she should recover and get home, she
would reproach the ministers for their neg-
lecting that sacrament, so plainly commanded
by St. James. In the afternoon, after she
had begged pardon for her wavering, and the
Catholick confession of faith was read aloud to
her, in the hearing of Mr. Craston, Mrs. Stilson, and another Englishwoman, she owned
the same. About seven o'clock the same day,
she said to Mr. Dubison, Shall not they give
me the holy communion? But her tongue
was then so thick that she could hardly swal-
low any thing. She was then anointed with
holy oil: But before, she said to Mr. Meriel,
Why have you not yet, sir, forgiven my sins?
In the night following, that priest, and Mr.
Dubison,

Dubison, were continually by her; and sometimes praying to God in her name, and praying to the Virgin Mary, and other saints. She
said also, I believe all: I am very glad Christ
was offered to his Father for me. Six or
seven hours before she died, a crucifix was
showed to her by Mr. Dubison; she took it,
and laid it upon her heart, and kissed it; and
then the nuns hanged it with a pair of beads
upon her neck. A little before she died, Mr.
Dubison asked her to pray for him in heaven;
she promised him: So she gave up the ghost,
at ten of the clock, the 27th of November,
whilst the high mass was saying; she was soon
commended to the prayers. On the fourth
day of the week following she was buried,
after the mass had been said for her. She
was laid by Abigail Turbet. Jan. 23,
1705,-6."

I HAVE here transcribed the letter in the
very words of it, without the least alteration:
The same for substance was sent to several
other

other captives. When I had this letter, I presently knew it to be of Mr. Meriel's composing: But the messenger, who brought the letter, brought word that my son had embraced their religion. Afterwards, when some blamed him for letting me know of it, because (they said) they feared my sorrow would shorten my days; he told me, he thought with himself, that if he was in my case he should be willing to know the worst, and therefore told me, as he would have desired to have known if in my place. I thanked him, acknowledging it a favour to let me know of it; but the news was ready to overwhelm me with grief and sorrow. I made my complaint to God, and mourned before him; sorrow and anguish took hold upon me. I asked of God to direct me what to do, and how to write, and find out an opportunity of conveying a letter to him; and committed this difficulty to his providence. I now found a greater opposition to a patient, quiet, humble resignation to the will of God than I should
otherwise

otherwise have known, if not so tried. Here I thought of my afflictions and trials; my wife and two children killed, and many of my neighbours; and myself, so many of my children and friends in a popish captivity, separated from our children, not capable to come to them to instruct them in the way they ought to go; and cunning, crafty enemies, using all their subtilty to insinuate into young ones such principles as would be pernicious. I thought with myself how happy many others were, in that they had their children with them, under all advantages to bring them up in the nurture and admonition of the Lord; whilst we were separated one from another, and our children in great peril of embracing damnable doctrines. Oh! that all parents, who read this history, would bless God for the advantages they have of educating their children, and faithfully improve it! I mourned when I thought with myself that I had one child with the Macquas, a second turned to popery, and a little child, of six years of age, in
danger

danger from a child to be instructed in popery; and knew full well that all endeavours would be used to prevent my seeing or speaking with them. But in the midst of all these, God gave me a secret hope, that he would magnify his power and free grace, and disappoint all their crafty designs. When I looked on the right hand and on the left, all refuge failed me, and none shewed any care for my soul. But God brought that word to uphold me; *Who is able to do exceeding abundantly above what we can ask or think.* As also that, *Is any thing too hard for God?* I prayed to God to direct me; and wrote very short the first time, and in general terms, fearing lest if I should write about things in controversy, my letters would not come to him. I therefore addressed him with the following letter.

"*Son Samuel,*

"YOURS of January 23, I received, and with it had the tidings that you had made an abjuration of the Protestant faith for the Romish: News that I heard with the most distressing,

tressing, afflicting, sorrowful spirit that ever I heard any news. Oh! I pity you, I mourn over you day and night! Oh! I pity your weakness, that through the craftiness of man you are turned from the simplicity of the gospel! I persuade myself you have done it through ignorance. Oh! why have you neglected to ask a father's advice in an affair of so great importance as the change of religion! God knows that the catechism, in which I instructed you is according to the word of God; and so will be found in the day of judgment. Oh! consider and bethink yourself what you have done! And whether you ask me or not, my poor child, I cannot but pray for you, that you may be recovered out of the snare you are taken in. Read the Bible, pray in secret; make Christ's righteousness your only plea before God, for justification: Beware of all immorality, and of profaning God's Sabbaths. Let a father's advice be asked for the future, in all things of weight and moment. What is a man profited if he gain the whole world, and lose

lose his own soul? Or what shall a man give in exchange for his soul? I desire to be humbled under the mighty hand of God thus afflicting of me. I would not do as you have done for ten thousand worlds. My heart aches within me, but I will yet wait upon the Lord: to Him will I commit your case day and night: He can perform all things for me and mine; and can yet again recover you from your fall. He is a God forgiving iniquity, transgression and sin: To the Lord our God belong forgivenesses, though we have rebelled. I charge you not to be instrumental to ensnare your poor brother Warham, or any other, and so add sin to sin. Accept of my love, and do not forsake a father's advice, who above all things desires that your soul may be saved in the day of the Lord."

WHAT I mournfully wrote, I followed with my poor cries to God in heaven to make effectual, to cause in him a consideration of what he had done. God saw what a proud
heart

heart I had, and what need I had to be so answered out of the whirlwind, that I might be humbled before him. Not having any answer to my letter for some weeks, I wrote the following letter, as I was enabled of God, and sent to him by a faithful hand; which, by the blessing of God, was made effectual for his good, and the good of others, who had fallen to popery; and for the establishing and strengthening of others to resist the essays of the adversary to truth. God brought good out of this evil, and made what was designed to promote their interests, an occasion of shame to them.

"*Son Samuel,*

"I HAVE waited till now for an answer from you, hoping to hear from you, why you made an abjuration of the Protestant faith for the Romish. But since you continue to neglect to write to me about it, as you neglected to take any advice or counsel from a father, when you did it, I cannot forbear writing again, and making some reflections
on

on the letter you wrote me last, about the two women. It seems to me, from those words of Abigail Turbet's, in your letter, or rather of Mr. Meriel's, which you transcribed for him [Abigail Turbet sent for Mr. Meriel, committed her soul into his hand, and was ready to do whatsoever he pleased]—I say, it seems rational to believe, that she had not the use of her reason; it is an expression to be abhorred by all who have any true sense of religion. Was Mr. Meriel a God, a Christ? Could he bear to hear such words and not reject them; replying, "Do not commit your soul into my hands, but see that you commit your soul into the hands of God through Christ Jesus, and do whatever God commands you in his holy word. As for me, I am a creature, and cannot save your soul; but will tell you of Acts iv. 12. *Neither is there salvation in any other; for there is no other name under heaven given among men, whereby we must be saved.*" Had he been a faithful minister of Jesus Christ, he would have said, "It is an honour
due

due to Christ alone. The holy apostle says, *Now unto him that is able to keep you, and present you faultless before the presence of his glory, with exceeding joy, to the only wise God our Saviour, be glory, and majesty, dominion and power, both now and ever, amen.*" Jude, 24, 25, verses. As to what you write about praying to the Virgin Mary, and other saints, I make this reply, Had Mr. Meriel done his duty, he would have said to them, as 1 John, ii. 1, 2. *If any man sin, we have an advocate with the Father, Jesus Christ the righteous; and he is the propitiation for our sins.* The Scriptures say, *There is one God, and one mediator between God and man, the man Christ Jesus.* Yea, Christ said, go and preach, *He that believeth and is baptized, shall be saved.* The apostle, in Gal. i. 8. saith, *But though we or an angel from heaven preach any other gospel unto you, than that we have preached to you, let him be accursed.* They never preached, that we should pray to the Virgin Mary, or other saints. As you would

would be saved, hear what the apostle saith,
Heb. iv. 13, &c. *Neither is there any creature
that is not manifest in his sight; but all things
are naked, and open unto the eyes of him
with whom we have to do. Seeing then that we
have a great high priest that is entered into
the heavens, Jesus the son of God, let us hold
fast our profession: For we have not an high
priest that cannot be touched with the feelings
of our infirmities, but was in all points tempted
like as we are, yet without sin; let us therefore
come boldly unto the throne of grace, that we
may obtain mercy, and find grace to help in
time of need.* Which words do hold forth,
how that Christ Jesus is in every respect qual-
ified to be a mediator and intercessor; and
I am sure they cannot be applied to any mere
creature, to make them capable of our religious trust.   When Roman Catholicks have
said all they can, they are not able to prove,
that the saints in heaven have a knowledge
of what prayers are directed to them.   Some
say they know them one way, others say they
have

have the knowledge of them in another way:
And that which they have fixed upon as most
probable to them, is, that they know of them
from their beholding the face of God; seeing
God, they know these prayers: But this is a
great mistake. Though the saints see and
know God in a glorious manner, yet they have
not an infinite knowledge; and it does no
ways follow, that because they see God, they
know all prayers that are directed to them
upon the earth. And God has no where in
his word told us, that the saints have such a
knowledge. Besides, were it a thing possible
for them to have a knowledge of what prayers
are directed to them, it does not follow that
they are to be prayed to, or have religious
honour conferred upon them. The Romanists can neither give one Scripture precept or
example for praying to them; but God has
provided a mediator, who knows all our
petitions, and is faithful and merciful enough
and we have both Scripture precept and
example, to look to him as our mediator and
advocate

advocate with the Father. Further, it cannot be proved that it is consistent with the
saints being creatures, as well as with their
happiness, to have a knowledge of prayers
from all parts of the world at the same time,
from many millions together, about things so
vastly differing one from another: And then
to present those supplications for all that look
to them, is not humility, but will-worship.
Col. ii. 18. *Let no man beguile you of your
reward, in a voluntary humility, worshipping
of angels,* verse 23. *Which things indeed have
a shew of wisdom and will-worship, and
humility.* For what humility can it be, to
distrust the way that God has provided and
encouraged us to come to him in, and impose
upon God a way of our own devising? Was
not God angry with Jeroboam for imposing
upon him after such a sort? 1 Kings, xii. 33.
*So he offered upon the altar which he had made
in Bethel, the fifth day of the eighth month,
which he devised of his own heart.* Therefore
Christ saith, Mark vii. 7. *Howbeit, in vain
                                             do*

do they worship me, teaching for doctrines the commandments of men. Before the coming of Christ, and his entering into heaven as an intercessor; Heb. vii. 25. *Wherefore he is able to save them to the uttermost that come to God by him, seeing he ever liveth to make intercession for them;* I say, before Christ's entering into heaven as an intercessor, there is not one word of any prayer to saints; and what reason can be given that now there is need of so many saints to make intercession when Christ as a priest is entered into heaven to make intercession for us? The answer that the Romanists give is a very fable and falsehood: Namely, that there were no saints in heaven till after the resurrection and ascension of Christ, but were reserved in a place called Limbus Patrum, and so had not the beatifical vision. See Gen. v. 24. *Enoch walked with God, and was not, for God took him.* If he was not taken into heaven, what can be the sense of those words, *for God took him?* Again, 2 Kings, ii. 1. When the Lord would

would take up Elijah into heaven by a whirlwind, verse 11. *There appeared a chariot
of fire and horses of fire, and parted them both
asunder, and Elijah went up by a whirlwind
into heaven.* Must the truth of the Scripture
be called in question to uphold their notions?
Besides, it is not consistent with reason to
suppose, that Enoch and Elias, instead of
having a peculiar privilege vouchsafed to
them, for their eminency in holiness, should
be less happy for so long a time than the rest
of the saints deceased, who are glorified in
heaven; which must be, if they are yet kept,
and must be, till the day of judgment out of
heaven, and the beatifical vision, in an
earthly paradise, according to some of the
Romanists; or in some other place, they know
not where, according to others. Religious
worship is not to be given to the creature,
Mat. iv. 9, 10, and saith, *All these things will
I give thee, if thou wilt fall down and worship
me.* Then saith Jesus to him, *Get thee
hence, Satan; for it is written, thou shalt
worship*

worship the Lord thy God, and him only shalt thou serve. That phrase, *and him only shalt thou serve,* excludes all creatures. Rev. xxii. 8, 9. *I fell down to worship before the feet of the angel, which shewed me these things; then saith he to me, see thou do it not, for I am thy fellow servant, and of thy brethren the prophets, and of them which keep the sayings of this book, worship God.* Which plainly shews, that God only is to be worshipped with a religious worship. None can think that Saint John intended to give the highest divine worship to the angel, who saith, *Do not fall down and worship me; it is God's due, worship God.* So Acts x. 25, 26. *As Peter was coming in, Cornelius met him and fell down at his feet, and worshipped him; but Peter took him up, saying, stand up, I myself also am a man.* See also Lev. xix. 10. The words of the second commandment (which the Romanists either leave out, or add to the first commandment, saying, *Thou shalt have no other gods before me,* adding, &c.) I say
the

the words of the second commandment are, *Thou shalt not make to thyself any graven image, or any likeness of any thing that is in heaven above, or that is in the earth beneath, or that is in the waters under the earth; thou shalt not bow down thyself to them nor serve them, for I the Lord thy God am a jealous God,* &c. These words being inserted in the letter which came from your brother Eleazer, in New-England, the last summer, was the cause of the letters being sent down from Montreal, and not given to you, when so near you, as I suppose, there being no other clause of the letter that could be objected against, and the reason why found at Quebec, when I sent it to you a second time, enclosed in a letter written by myself. The brazen serpent, made by divine appointment as a type of Christ, when abused to superstition, was by reforming Hezekiah broken in pieces. As to what the Romanists plead about the lawfulness of image and saint worship, from those likenesses of things made in Solomon's temple,

ple, it is nothing to the purpose. We do not
say it is not lawful to make or have a picture;
but those carved images were not, in the temple, to be adored, bowed down to, or worshipped. There is no manner of consequence,
that because there were images made in Solomon's temple that were not adored and
worshipped, that therefore it is now lawful
to make and fall down before images, and
pray to them, and so worship them.

"Religious worshipping of saints cannot
be defended from, but is forbidden, in the
Scriptures; and for fear of losing their disciples, the Romanists keep away from them
the Bible and oblige them to believe as they
say they must believe; as though there was no
use be made of our reason about our souls;
and yet the Bereans were counted noble for
searching the Scriptures, to see whether the
things preached by Saint Paul were so or not.
They dare not allow you liberty to speak
with your father, or others, for fear their
errors should be discovered to you. Again,
you

you write, "that Esther Jones confessed that
there was an inequality of power among the
pastors of the church." An argument to
convince the world, that because the priests,
in fallacious ways, caused a woman, distem-
pered with a very high fever, if not distracted,
to say, she confessed there was an inequality
of power among the pastors of the church,
therefore all the world are obliged to believe
that there is a pope. An argument to be
sent from Dan to Beersheba, every where,
where any English captives are, to gain their
belief of a pope. Can any rational man
think that Christ, in the 16th chapter of Matthew, gave Saint Peter such a power as the
papists speak of; or that the disciples so
understood Christ? When immediately there
arose a dispute among them, who should be
the greatest in the kingdom of heaven?
Matth. xviii. 1. *At the same time came the
disciples of Jesus, saying, who is the greatest
in the kingdom of heaven?* The rock spoken
of in the 16th of Matthew, not the person of
                                        Peter,

Peter, but the confession made by him, and
the same power is given to all the disciples,
if you compare one Scripture with another;
not one word in any place of Scripture of such
a vicarship power as of a pope, nor any solid
foundation of proof that Peter had a greater authority than the rest of the apostles.
I Cor. iv. 6. *That you might learn in us, not
to think of men above that which is written.*
Yea, the apostle condemns them, I Cor. i.
12. for their contentions, *One saying, I am
of Paul, I of Apollos, and I of Cæphas;* no
more of Peter's being a foundation than any
of the rest. *For we are built upon the foundation of the apostles and prophets, Jesus
Christ himself being the chief corner stone.*
Not one word in any of Peter's epistles, shewing that he had greater power than the other
apostles. Nay, if the Scriptures give any
preference, it is to Saint Paul rather than
Saint Peter. I Cor. iii. 10. *According to
the grace of God which is given to me, as a
wise master builder I have laid the foundation.*
I Cor.

I Cor. v. 3, 4. *For I verily as absent in body, but present in spirit, have judged already, as though I were present, concerning him that hath done so this deed. In the name of our Lord Jesus Christ, when ye are gathered together, and my spirit, with the power of our Lord Jesus Christ,* &c. I Cor. vii. 1. *Now concerning the things whereof ye wrote to me;* application made not to Saint Peter, but Paul, for the decision of a controversy or scruple. I Cor. xi. 2. *Now I praise you, brethren, that you remember me in all things, and keep the ordinances as I delivered them to you.* Either those spoken of, Acts xv. or in his ministry and epistles, 2 Cor. ii. 10. *For your sake, forgave I it, in the person of Christ.* 2 Cor. xi. 28. *That which cometh upon me daily, the care of all the churches.* 2 Cor. xii. 11, 12. *For in nothing am I behind the very chiefest of the apostles, though I be nothing. Truly the signs of an apostle were wrought among you in all patience, in signs and wonders, and mighty deeds;* and in other places.

Again,

Again, if you consult Acts xv. where you have
an account of the first synod or council, you
will find that the counsel or sentence of the
apostle James is followed, verse 19. Wherefore my sentence is, &c. not a word that
Saint Peter was chief. Again, you find Peter
himself sent forth by the other apostles,
Acts viii. 14. *The apostles sent unto them, Peter
and John.* When the church of the Jews found
fault with Peter, for going in to the Gentiles
when he went to Cornelius, he does not say,
— Why do you question me, or call me to an
account, I am Christ's vicar on earth. When
Paul reproved Peter, Gal. ii. he does not defend himself, by mentioning an infallibility
in himself as Christ's vicar, or reprove Paul
for his boldness.

"The Roman Catholick Church cannot be
a true church of Christ, in that it makes laws
directly contrary to the laws and commands
of Christ: As for example, in with-holding
the wine or the cup from the laity, in the
Lord's Supper; whereas Christ commands
the

the same to drink who were to eat. Their evasion, that the blood is in the body, and so they partake of both in eating, is a great fallacy, built on a false foundation of transubstantiation. For when men eat, they cannot be said to drink, which Christ commands, for Christ commands that we *take the cup and drink*, which is not done in eating; besides, the priests themselves will not be so put off. The words, *this is my body*, do only intend, *this doth signify or represent my body*, which will appear if you compare Scripture with Scripture; for after the consecration, the Holy Ghost calls it bread, and the fruit of the vine. Exod. xii. 11. *It is the Lord's passover;* that is, it represents it. In all the evangelists, you read of killing and eating the passover, a few lines or verses before these words, *this is my body*, which plainly shew, that our Saviour, in the same way of figurative expression, speaks of the gospel sacrament. If these words were taken as the Romanists expound them, he must eat his own body
himself,

himself, whole and entire in his own hands;
and after that, each one of the disciples eat
him entire, and yet he set at the table whole,
untouched, at the same time; contradictions
impossible to be defended by any rational arguments. Yea, his whole body must be now in
heaven and in a thousand other places, and in
the mouth of every communicant at the same
time, and that both as a broken and unbroken
sacrifice, and be subject to putrefaction.
Christ is said to be a door, a true vine, a way,
a rock. What work shall we make if we expound these in a literal manner, as the Romanists do, when they say, *this is my body*, means
the real body of Christ in the eucharist? It
is said, 1 Cor. x. 4. *And did all drink the same
spiritual drink: For they drank of that spiritual Rock that followed them: And that rock
was Christ.* Was Christ literally a rock,
think you? Yea, it is absurd to believe, that
a priest, uttering a few words over a wafer
not above an inch square, can make it a God,
or the body of Christ entire, as it was offered
on

on the cross. It is a blasphemy to pretend to a power of making God at their pleasure; and then eat him, and give him to others to be eaten, or shut him up in their altars: That they can utter the same words, and make a God or not make a God, according to their intention, and that the people are obliged to believe that it is God, and so adore it, when they never hear any word of consecration, nor know the priest's intention.

"As to what you write about the holy mass, I reply, it is wholly an human invention; not a word of such a sacrifice in the whole Bible; its being a sacrifice propitiatory daily to be offered, is contrary to the holy Scriptures. Heb. vii. 27. *Who needeth not daily, as those high-priests, to offer up sacrifice first for his own sins, and then for the people's: For this he did once, when he offered up himself.* And yet the Romanists say, there is need that he be offered up as a sacrifice to God every day. Heb. ix. 12. *By his own blood he entered in once into the holy place,*

place, having obtained eternal redemption for us. ver. 25, 26, 27, 28. *Nor yet that he should offer himself often, as the high-priest entereth into the holy place, every year, with the blood of others: For then must he often have suffered since the foundation of the world. But now once, in the end of the world, hath he appeared to put away sin by the sacrifice of himself. As it is appointed unto men once to die, but after this the judgment; so Christ was once offered to bear the sins of many.* Heb. x. 10. *By which will we are sanctified, through the offering of the body of Jesus Christ once for all.* ver. 12. *But this man, after he had offered one sacrifice for sins, forever sat down on the right-hand of God.* ver. 14. *For by one offering he hath perfected forever them that are sanctified.* By which Scriptures you may see, that the mass is not of divine appointment, but an human invention. Their evasion of a bloody and an unbloody sacrifice, is a sham; the holy Scriptures speak not one word of Christ's being

being offered as a sacrifice propitiatory, after
such a sort as they call an unbloody sacrifice. All the ceremonies of the mass are
human   inventions,   which   God   never
commanded.

"As to what is in the letter about praying
for the women after their death, it is very
ridiculous. For as the tree falls, so it lies;
as death leaves, judgment will find. No
change after death from an afflicted to a
happy place and state. Purgatory is a
phantasm, for enriching the clergy, and impoverishing the laity. The notion of it is a
fatal snare to many souls, who sin with hopes
of easily getting priestly absolutions at death,
and buying off torments with their money.
The soul at death goes immediately to judgment, and so to heaven or hell. No authen-
tick place of Scripture mentions so much as
one word of any such place or state. Mr.
Meriel told me, "If I found one error in our
religion, it was enough to cause me to disown
our whole religion." By his argument, you
may

may see what reason you have to avoid that
religion that is so full of errors. Bethink
yourself, and consult the Scriptures, if you
can get them: (I mean the Bible). Can you
think their religion is right when they are
afraid to let you have an English Bible? Or to
speak with your father, or other of your
Christian neighbours, for fear they should
give you such convictions of truth that they
cannot remove? Can that religion be true,
that cannot bear an examination from the
Scriptures, which are a perfect rule in matters
of faith? Or that must he upheld by ignorance, especially ignorance of the holy
Scriptures?

"These things have I written, as in my
heart I believe. I long for your recovery,
and will not cease to pray for it. I am now
a man of a sorrowful spirit, and look upon
your fall as the most aggravating circumstance of my afflictions, and am persuaded
that no pains will be wanting to prevent me
from seeing or speaking with you; but I
know

know that God's grace is all-sufficient. He is able to do exceeding abundantly above what I can ask or think. Do not give way to discouragement as to a return to New-England; read over what I have written, and keep it with you if you can; you have no friend on earth that wisheth your eternal salvation more heartily than your father. I long to see and speak with you, but I never forget you; my love to you, and to your brother and sister, and to all our fellow-prisoners. Let me hear from you as often as you can. I hope God will appear for us before it be long.

"There are a great many other things in the letter, which deserve to be refuted; but I shall be too tedious in remarking on them all at once: Yet would not pass over that passage in the letter in which Esther Jones confessed that there were seven sacraments. To which I answer, That some of the most learned of the Romish religion confessed, (without the distracting pains of a violent fever), and left

it

it upon record in print, that it cannot be con-
vincingly made out from the Scriptures, that
there are seven sacraments, and that their
most incontestable proof is from tradition,
and by their traditions they might have found
seventeen as well as seven; considering that
four popes, successively, spent their lives in
purging and correcting old authors. But no
man can, out of the holy Scriptures, prove
any more than two sacraments of divine in-
stitution, under the New-Testament, namely,
baptism and the Lord's Supper. If you make
the Scriptures a perfect rule of faith, as you
ought to do, you cannot believe as the Roman
Church believes. Oh! see that you sanctify the Lord himself in your heart, and make
him your fear and your dread. Fear not
them that can kill the body, and after that
have no more that they can do; but rather
fear him that has power to destroy soul and
body in hell fire. The Lord have mercy upon
you, and shew you mercy, for the worthiness
and righteousness sake of Jesus Christ, our
                                              great

great and glorious Redeemer and Advocate, who makes intercession for transgressors. My prayers are daily offered to God for you, for your brother and sister, yea for all my children, and fellow prisoners.

"I am your afflicted and sorrowful father,

"JOHN WILLIAMS.

"Chateauviche, March 22, 1706."

GOD, who is gloriously free and rich in his grace to vile sinners, was pleased to bless poor and weak means for the recovery of my child so taken, and gave me to see, that he did not say to the house of Jacob, Seek you me in vain. Oh! that every reader would in every difficulty make him their refuge; he is a hopeful stay. To alleviate my sorrow, I received the following letter in answer to mine.

Montreal, May 12, 1706.

"*Honoured Father,*

"I RECEIVED your letter which you sent by ——, which good letter I thank you for; and for the good counsel which you gave me:

me: I desire to be thankful for it, and hope
it will be for the good of my soul.   I may
say as in the Psalms: *The sorrows of death
compassed me, and the pains of hell gat hold
on me: I found trouble and sorrow, then called
I upon the name of the Lord: O Lord, I beseech thee, deliver my soul! Gracious is the
Lord and righteous, yea our God is merciful.*
As for what you ask me about my making
an abjuration of the Protestant faith for the
Romish, I durst not write so plain to you
as I would, but hope to see and discourse
with you.   I am sorry for the sin I have committed in changing of religion, for which I
am greatly to blame.   You may know, that
Mr. Meriel, the school-master, and others,
were continually at me about it; at last I
gave over to it; for which I am very sorry.
As for that letter you had from me, it was a
letter I had transcribed for Mr. Meriel: And
for what he saith about Abigail Turbet, and
Esther Jones, no body heard them but he, as
I understand.   I desire your prayers to God
for

for me, to deliver me from my sins. Oh
remember me in your prayers! I am your
dutiful son, ready to take your counsel.

"SAMUEL WILLIAMS."

THIS priest, Mr. Meriel, has brought
many letters to him, and bid him write them
over and send them, and so he has done for
many others. By this, as also by Mrs.
Stilson's saying, "She does not think that
either of these women did change their religion
before their death;" and also, "oftentimes
during their sickness, whilst they had the use
of their reason, they protested against the Romish religion and faith," it is evident that
these women never died papists, but that
it was a wily stratagem of the priests to advance their religion: For letters were sent immediately, after their death, to use this as a
persuasive argument to gain others. But
God in his providence gave further conviction
of their fallaciousness in this matter.

For the last summer, one Biggilow, of Marlborough,

borough, a captive at Montreal, was very
sick in the hospital, and, in the judgment
of all, with a sickness to death. Then the
priests and others gave out, that he was turned
to be of their religion, and taken into their communion: But, contrary to their expectations,
he was brought back from the gates of death,
and would comply with none of their rites;
saying, that whilst he had the use of his
reason, he never spake anything in favour of
their religion; and that he never disowned
the Protestant faith, nor would he now. So
that they were silenced and put to shame.
There is no reason to think that these two
women were any more papists than he; but
they are dead, and cannot speak. One of the
witnesses, spoken of in the fore-mentioned
letter, told me, she knew of no such thing,
and said Mr. Meriel told her, that he never
heard a more fervent and affectionate prayer
than one which Esther Jones made a little
before her death. I am verily persuaded,
that he calls that prayer to God, so full of

affection

affection and confession, the confession made
by her of the sins of her whole life. These
two women always in their health, and so in
their sickness, opposed all popish principles,
as all that knew them can testify, so long as
they could be permitted to go and speak with
them. One of these women was taken from
the eastward, and the other, namely, Esther
Jones, from Northampton.

In the beginning of March, 1706, Mr. Sheldon came again to Canada, with letters from
his excellency our governour, at which time
I was a few days at Quebec. And when I
was there, one night about ten o'clock, there
was an earthquake, that made a report like
a cannon, and made the houses to tremble:
It was heard and felt many leagues, all along
the island of St. Laurence, and other places.
When Mr. Sheldon came the second time,
the adversaries did what they could to retard
the time of our return, to gain time to seduce
our young ones to popery. Such were sent
away who were judged ungainable, and most
of

of the younger sort still kept.   Some were still
flattered with promises of reward; and great
essays made to get others married among
them.   One was debauched, and then in
twenty-four hours of time published, taken
into their communion and married; but the
poor soul has had time since to lament her
sin and folly, with a bitter cry; and asks your
prayers, that God of his sovereign grace would
yet bring her out of the horrible pit she has
thrown herself into.   Her name was Rachel
Storer, of Wells.

In April, one Zebediah Williams, of our
town, died: He was a very hopeful and pious
young man, who carried himself so in his
captivity, as to edify several of the English,
and recover one fallen to popery, taken the
last war; though some were enraged against
him on these accounts; yet even the
French, where he sojourned, and with whom
he conversed, would say he was a good man:
One that was very prayerful to God, and
studious and painful in reading the holy
Scriptures:

Scriptures: A man of a good understanding, and desirable conversation. In the beginning of his last sickness, he made me a visit, (before he went to the hospital at Quebec), as he had several times before, to my great satisfaction and our mutual consolation and comfort in our captivity. He lived not above two miles from me, over the river, at the island of St. Laurence, about six week or two months. After his death, the French told me, Zebediah was gone to hell, and damned: For, said they, he has appeared, since his death, to one Joseph Egerly, an Englishman, who was taken the last war, in flaming fire, telling him, "he was damned for refusing to embrace the Romish religion, when such pains were used to bring him to the true faith, and for being instrumental to draw him away from the Romish communion, forsaking the mass; and was therefore now come to advertise him of his danger." I told them I judged it to be a popish lie; saying, I bless God our religion needs no lies to uphold,

maintain,

maintain, and establish it, as theirs did. But
they affirmed it to be true, telling me, how God
approved of their religion, and witnessed
miraculously against ours. But I still told
them, I was persuaded his soul was in heaven,
and that these reports were only devised
fables to seduce souls. For several weeks
they affirmed it, telling me, that all who came
over the river from the island affirmed it to
be a truth. I begged of God to blast this
hellish design of theirs, so that in the issue
it might be to render their religion more
abominable, and that they might not gain
one soul by such a stratagem. After some
weeks had passed in such assertions, there
came one into my landlord's house, affirming it to be a truth reported of Zebediah,
saying, Joseph Egerly had been over the river,
and told one of our neighbours this story.
After a few hours I saw that neighbour, and
asked him whether he had seen Egerly
lately; he said, Yes; What news told he to
you ? None, said he. Then I told him what was
affirmed

affirmed as a truth; he answered, Egerly said
nothing like this to him, and he was persuaded
he would have told him, if there had been
any truth in it. About a week after this,
came one John Boult from the island of St.
Laurence, a lad taken from Newfoundland, a
very serious, sober lad, of about seventeen
years of age; he had often before come over
with Zebediah to visit me.   At his coming in,
he much lamented the loss of Zebediah, and
told me, "That for several weeks they had
told him the same story, affirming it to be
a truth, and that Egerly was so awakened
by it, as to go again to mass every day;"
urging him, "since God, in such a miraculous way, offered such conviction of the
truth of their religion, and the falsehood and
danger of ours, to come over to their religion,
or else his damnation would be dreadfully
aggravated."   He said, "he could have no
rest for them day and night," but (said
he) "I told them their religion was contrary
to the word of God, and therefore I would
                                                    not

not embrace it; and that I did not believe
what they said." And says he to me, "One
day I was sitting in the house, and Egerly
came in, and I spake to him before the whole
family (in the French tongue, for he could
not speak much English) and asked him of
this story; he answered, it is a great falsehood, saying, he never appeared to me, nor
have I ever reported any such thing to any
body; and that he had never been at mass
since Zebediah's death." At the hearing of
which, they were silenced and put to shame.
We blessed God together, for discovering
their wickedness, and disappointing them at
what they aimed at, and prayed to God to deliver us and all the captives from delusions, and
recover them who had fallen, and so parted.
After which I took my pen and wrote a letter
to one Mr. Samuel Hill, an English captive,
taken from Wells, who lived at Quebec, and
his brother Ebenezer Hill, to make a discov-
ery of this lying plot, to warn them of their
danger, and assure them of the falsehood of
this

this report; but the letter fell into the hands
of the priests, and was never delivered. This
Egerly came home with us, so that they
gained nothing but shame by this stratagem.
God often dissappoints the crafty devices
of wicked men.

In the latter end of summer, they told me,
"they had news from New-England, by one
who had been a captive at Boston, who said
that the ministers at Boston had told the
French captives, that the Protestant religion
was the only true religion; and that as a confirmation of it, they would raise a dead person to life before their eyes, for their conviction; and that having persuaded one to feign
himself dead, they came and prayed over
him, and then commanded him in the name
of Christ, (whose religion they kept pure) to
arise; they called and commanded, but he
never arose; so that instead of raising the
dead, they killed the living; which the be-
reaved relations discovered." I told them,
"it was an old lie and calumny against
Luther

Luther and Calvin, new vamped, and that they
only change the persons and place;" but they
affirmed it to be a truth: I told them, "I
wondered they were so fond of a faith propa-
gated, and then maintained by lying words."

We were always out of hopes of being returned before winter, the season proving so
cold in the latter end of September, and were
praying to God to prepare our hearts, with an
holy submission to his holy will, to glorify
his holy name in a way of passive obedience
in the winter. For my own part, I was informed by several who came from the city,
that the lord intendant said, if More returned,
and brought word that Battis was in prison,
he would put me into prison, and lay me in
irons. They would not permit me to go into
the city, saying, I always did harm when I
came to the city, and if at any time I was at
the city, they would persuade the governour
to send me back again.

In the beginning of last June, the superiour
of the priests came to the parish where I was,
and

and told me, he saw I wanted my friend Captain de Beauville, and that I was ragged. But, says he, your obstinacy against our religion discourages from providing better clothes. I told him, it was better going in a ragged coat, than with a ragged conscience.

In the beginning of last June, went out an army of five hundred Macquas and Indians, with an intention to have fallen on some English towns down Connecticut river; but lighting on a Scatacook Indian, who afterwards ran away in the night, they were discouraged; saying, he would alarm the whole country. About fifty, as some say, or eighty, as others, returned. Thus God restrained their wrath.

When they were promising themselves another winter, to draw away the English to popery, came news that an English brigantine was coming, and that the honourable Capt. Samuel Appleton, Esq. was coming ambassador, to fetch off the captives, and Capt. John Bonner with him. I cannot tell you how

how the clergy and others laboured to stop
many of the prisoners. To some, liberty;
to others, money and yearly pensions, were
offered, if they would stay. Some they urged
to tarry at least till the spring of the year, telling them, it was so late in the year, they would
be lost by ship-wreck if they went now; some
younger ones they told, if they went home,
they would be damned, and burn in hell
forever, to affright them. Day and night
they were urging of them, to stay. And I
was threatened to be sent abroad, without a
permission to come ashore again, if I should
again discourse with any of the English who
were turned to their religion. At Montreal,
especially, all crafty endeavours were used
to stay the English. They told my child, if
he would stay, he should have an honourable
pension from the king every year; and that
his master, who was an old man, and the
richest in Canada, would give him a great
deal; telling him, if he returned he would be
poor, for (said they) your father is poor, has
                                               lost

lost all his estate, it was all burnt. But he would not be prevailed with to stay. Others were also in like manner urged to stay; but God graciously brake the snare, and brought them out. They endeavoured, in the fall of the year, to prevail with my son to go to France, when they saw he would not come to their communion any more. One woman, belonging to the eastern parts, who had, by their persuasions, married an English captive, taken the last war, came away with her husband, which made them say, they were sorry they ever persuaded her to turn to their religion, and then to marry. For instead of advancing their cause by it, they had weakened it; for now they had not only lost her, but another they thought they had made sure of. Another woman, belonging to the eastward, who had been flattered to their religion, to whom a Bible was denied, till she promised to embrace their religion, and then had the promise of it for a little time, opening her Bible whilst in the church, and present at

mass,

mass, she read the fourth chapter of Deuteronomy, and received such conviction whilst reading, that before her first communion, she fell off from them, and could never be prevailed with any more to be of their religion.

We have reason to bless God, who has wrought deliverance for so many, and yet to pray to God for a door of escape to be opened for the great number yet behind, not much short of an hundred, many of whom are children, and of these not a few among the savages; and having lost the English tongue, will be lost, and turn savages in a little time, unless something extraordinary prevent.

The vessel that came for us, in its voyage to Canada, struck on a bar of sands, and there lay in very great hazard for four tides; and yet they saw reason to bless God for striking there; for had they got over that bar, they would at midnight, in a storm of snow, have run upon a terrible ledge of rocks.

We came away from Quebec on October 25; and by contrary winds and a great storm,
we

we were retarded, and then driven back near
the city, and had a great deliverance from
shipwreck, the vessel striking twice on a rock
in that storm.   But through God's goodness,
we all arrived in safety at Boston, November
21; the number of captives fifty-seven, two of
whom were my children.   I have yet a daughter of ten years of age, and many neighbours
whose case bespeaks your compassion, and
prayers to God to gather them, being out-
casts ready to perish.

At our arrival at Boston, we found the
kindnesses of the Lord in a wonderful manner, in God's opening the hearts of many, to
bless God with us and for us, wonderfully to
give for our supplies in our needy state.   We
are under obligations to praise God, for disposing the hearts of so many to so great charity, and under great bonds to pray for a blessing on the heads, hearts and families of them,
who so liberally and plentifully gave for our
relief.   It is certain, that the charity of the
whole country of Canada, though moved with
the

the doctrines of merit, does not come up to the charity of Boston alone, where notions of merit are rejected; but acts of charity performed out of a right Christian spirit, from a spirit of thankfulness to God, out of obedience to God's command, and unfeigned love and charity to them that are of the same family and household of faith. The Lord grant, that all who devise such liberal things, may find the accomplishment of the promises made by God, in their own persons, and theirs after them, from generation to generation.

I SHALL annex a short account of the troubles beginning to arise in Canada. On May 16, arrived a canoe at Quebec, which brought letters from Mississippi, written the May preceeding, giving an account that the plague was there, and that one hundred and fifty French, in a very little time, had died of it; and that the savages, called the Lezilouways, were very turbulent, and had with their arrows wounded a Jesuit in five places, and killed a Frenchman that waited on him. In July, news came, that the nations up the river were engaged in a war one against the other, and that the French living so among them, and trading with them, were in great danger; that
the

the Mitchelmacquinas had made war with the Mizian-
mies, and had killed a mendicant friar, and three other
Frenchmen, and eleven savages, at a place called the
straits, where they are settling a garrison and place for
traffick; the Mitchelmacquinas had taken sixteen Frenchmen prisoners, and burnt their trading houses. These
tidings made the French very full of perplexing troubles;
but the Jesuits are endeavouring to pacify them; but the
troubles, when we came away, were rather encreasing
than lessening; for the last letters from the French prisoners at Mitchel-macquina* report, that the savages had
sent out two companies, one of an hundred and fifty,
another of an hundred and sixty, against the savages at
the straits; and they feared, they would engage as well
against the French as the Indians.

THE END.

---

*The present *Mackinaw*, on the *Strait* of *Mackinac*, or *Mackinaw*,
formerly *Michilimackinac*, between Lakes Michigan and Huron.

Reports of Divine Kindness; or Remarkable Mercies should be faithfully published, for the Praise of God the Giver;

SET FORTH IN A

SERMON,

PREACHED AT BOSTON LECTURE, *December* 5, 1706.

BY JOHN WILLIAMS,

Pastor of the CHURCH of CHRIST in *Deerfield,* soon after his Return from Captivity.

PSALM cvii. 13, 14, 15, 32. *He saved them out of their distresses. He brought them out of darkness, and the shadow of death; and brake their bands in sunder. O that men would praise the Lord for his goodness; and for his wonderful works to the children of men.—Let them exalt him also in the congregation of the people, and praise him in the assembly of the elders.*
PSALM xxxiv. 3. *O magnify the Lord with me, and let us exalt his name together.*

LUKE VIII. 39.

Return to thine own house, and shew how great things GOD hath done unto thee.—

T H E infinitely wise disposer of all things, who aims at his own glory, in the governing
of

of rational creatures, doth sometimes bring
persons into the depths of distress; and then
magnify his power and grace in raising them
up out of their afflictions: And in many respects, by such things, he has a design of advancing his own honour and glory in the
world. We find in the context, a person in a
very doleful, distressed condition: He seems
to be forsaken of God, and made a possession
and dwelling place of evil spirits, deprived
of all human comforts and delights, made
to possess sorrow and pain to such a degree,
as to be a common subject or theme of discourse for all men to relate doleful things
about. And afterward, God, in very remarkable and wonderful works of power
and mercy, not only gives release from his
sorrowful possession, but he is sitting at the
feet of Jesus, cloathed, and in his right mind.
Now this was done for the declarative and
manifestative glory and honour of God. For
when this man, for whom such great things
had been done, petitions Christ that he may
abide

abide with him, to hear from him, and pay
his respects to him; he receives commandment, to be glorifying the power and mercy
of God, in declaring to others what great
things God had done for him.

1. A subject of great mercy; or a person
spoken of, for whom God had done great
things, bestowed eminent mercies.

2. A particular and special command
from Christ, to be glorifying God in relating
to others, what mercies he had been the subject of.

3. His obedience to the great command
of Christ. He went and published the great
things done for him by Christ; so that from
the command of Christ, and his obedience
to it, for which he is commended, you may
observe this doctrinal conclusion.

Doct. It well becomes those who have had
eminent mercies, to be shewing to others
what great things God has done for them.

The holy Scriptures, in many places,
confirm

confirm this truth. See Exod. xii. 25, 26, 27.
*And it shall come to pass, when ye be come to the
land, which the Lord will give you, accord̦ing
as he hath promised, that ye shall keep this
service. And it shall come to pass, when your
children shall say unto you, what mean you
by this service? That ye shall say, it is the
sacrifice of the Lord's passover, who passed
over the houses of the children of Israel in
Egypt, when he smote the Egyptians, and delivered our houses.* Exod. xiii. 8, 10. *And
thou shalt shew thy son in that day, saying,
this is done because of that which the Lord did
unto me, when I came forth out of Egypt. Thou
shalt therefore keep this ordinance in his season from year to year.* Psal. lxxviii. 3, 4.
*Which we have heard and known, and our
fathers have told us; we will not hide them
from our children, shewing to the generation
to come the praises of the Lord; and his strength,
and his wonderful works that he hath done.*
In the prosecution and handling of this
truth, consider,

I. They

I. They who have had mercies, have had them from God. God is the bestower and giver of all our good things: All our mercies come to us by a divine providence, and ordering; not by casualty or accident: Neither are they of our own procuring and purchasing, or others, so as to exclude the providential disposing of God. It is God who returns the captivity of Zion, Psalm cxxvi. begin. *When the Lord turned again the captivity of Zion, we were like them that dream: Then was our mouth filled with laughter, and our tongue with singing. Then said they among the heathen, the Lord hath done great things for them. The Lord hath done great things for us; whereof we are glad: Turn again our captivity, O Lord.* The very heathen acknowledge the good things bestowed upon, and done for the church, to be from God; and God's own people acknowledge him for the mercies granted, and humbly supplicate mercies from him for the future. It is God who gathers the out-casts of Israel: It is he who
takes

takes away the captives of the mighty, the
prey of the terrible; who contends with them
that contend with us, and saves our children.
It is God who disperseth and gathers again:
Therefore the psalmist, Psal. ciii. bigin. calls
upon his soul to bless the Lord, and not to
forget all his benefits: and saith, *It is God
who forgiveth all thy iniquities, who healeth
all thy diseases: Who redeemeth thy life from
destruction, who crowneth thee with loving
kindness and tender mercies,* &c. Sometimes
God, in a more immediate and extraordinary
way and manner, confers blessings and mercies; sometimes in a more ordinary and
mediate way; but his providence is to be
acknowledged in all: Not one single mercy
comes to us, without a commission from that
God by whom our very hairs are numbered.

II. It well becomes those who have had
eminent mercies, to be shewing to others what
great things God hath done for them. Therefore you find the holy psalmist calling upon
others, to give a listening ear, whilst he makes
a narration

a narration of the salvations he had from God, Psal. lxvi. 16. *Come and hear, all you that fear God, and I will declare what he hath done for my soul.*

1*st* *Reason.* Because God aimed at the advancement of his own honour and glory, in the giving and dealing out of these mercies. God makes and disposeth all things for his own honour and glory. All works of providence are some way or other to advance the honour and glory of God in the world. The glory of his power, wisdom, mercy, justice and holiness, are some way or other advanced in a declarative and manifestative way and manner. Now it well becomes us to fall in with the design of God, and in an active manner to be giving him glory. That God designs to have glory given to him, is evident from Psal. l. 15. *And call upon me in the day of trouble, I will deliver thee, and thou shalt glorify me.* Exod. vii. 5. *And the Egyptians shall know that I am the Lord, when I stretch forth mine hand upon Egypt, and*
                                         bring

*bring out the children of Israel from among
them.* God has a design to magnify his
power, mercy and covenant faithfulness, in
the eyes of the world.

2d Reason. Because God has given us
direct precepts, and positive commands, in
this way, to be glorifying of him. God is
our Lord and lawgiver, and he requires, that
among other ways of shewing forth his praises
we do it by rehearsing his praise-worthy acts
to the children of men: So that in obedience
to God, and answering that high and noble
end we were made for, it is requisite that in
this way we glorify God. It is enough, that
the great God, who hath taken us into covenant relation to himself, has enjoined us
to shew forth his praises, in rehearsing to
others the salvations and favours we have
been the subjects of. The forementioned
Scriptures, with many others that might be
enumerated, sufficiently demonstrate, that
God calls for our thankful acknowledgments in this way; and upon the account of
this

this being so agreeable to the revealed and perceptive will of God, the psalmist expresseth himself, as in Psal. cxlv. 4, 5, 6. *One generation shall praise thy works to another, and shall declare thy mighty acts. I will speak of the glorious honour of thy majesty, and of thy wondrous works. And men shall speak of the might of thy terrible acts: And I will declare thy greatness. They shall abundantly utter the memory of thy great goodness; and shall sing of thy righteousness.* Verses 10, 11, 12. *All thy works shall praise thee, O Lord; and thy saints shall bless thee. They shall speak of the glory of thy kingdom, and talk of thy power: To make known to the sons of men his mighty acts, and the glorious majesty of his kingdom.*

3d Reason. Because hereby they will stir up others to bless God with them, and for them. A truly gracious soul finds by experience, that he can do but a little in glorifying God, and finds how far he falls short of the rule of duty in so reasonable a service

as

as glorifying God. / And being enlarged in desires that the glory due to God might be given him, doth call upon others to join with him in this heavenly service of praising God; and therefore tells them what great things God has done. Psalm xxxiv. 2, 3, 4, 6. *My soul shall make her boast in the Lord: The humble shall hear thereof, and be glad. O magnify the Lord with me, and let us exalt his name together. I sought the Lord, and he heard me; and delivered me from all my fears. This poor man cried, and the Lord heard him; and saved him out of all his troubles.* When Moses told his father-in-law Jethro, the great things God had done for Israel, he glorifies God on their hehalf, Exod. xviii. 8, &c. *And Moses told his father-in-law, all that the Lord had done unto Pharaoh, and to the Egyptians for Israel's sake, and all the travail that had come upon them by the way, and how the Lord delivered them. And Jethro rejoiced for all the goodness which the Lord had done to Israel; whom he had delivered*

out

*out of the hand of the Egyptians. And Jethro
said, blessed be the Lord, who hath delivered
you out of the hand of the Egyptians,
and out of the hand of Pharaoh, who hath
delivered the people from under the hand of
the Egyptians. Now I know that the Lord
is greater than all gods: For in the thing wherein
they dealt proudly, he was above them.* By
this means, thanks will be given to God by
many: As many have been praying to God for
them, so many will be praising and blessing
God with them and for them.

4th Reason. Because hereby they will
oftentimes be advised and counselled how to
improve such mercies to the glory of God.
We are conscious to ourselves of so much
blindness, ignorance, and darkness, that we
cannot but own it a great thing to be in a
way for the best counsel, what to do with our
mercies, and what and how to return to God
for them. Now the publishing the great
things done by God for us, puts others in a
capacity to be advising and telling us what
temptations

temptations we may expect to meet with, and what will be needful on our part to avoid temptations, and how to over-come; they will be counselling us, how to be in a way of rendering to the Lord according to the benefits done unto us; what duties God looks for the performance of, and directions how to do duty. In a word, we may be counselled how to order our whole conversation so as God may have glory, and our good purposes of honouring and glorifying God with our mercies, established. Prov. xx. 18. *Every purpose is established by counsel.* When Moses had told Jethro what great things God had done for Israel, he saith, Exod. xviii. 19. *Hearken now unto my voice, I will give thee counsel, and God shall be with thee, &c.*

5th Reason. Because hereby they will be instrumental to put others upon trusting God, making him their hope and refuge in an evil day. Others will be excited to a seeking refuge under the shadow of his wings, Psal. xliv. begin. *We have heard with our ears, O God,*

O God, our fathers have told us, what work thou didst in their days, in the times of old. How thou didst drive out the heathen, &c. And then it is said, *Thou art my king, O God: Command deliverances for Jacob. Through thee will we push down our enemies: Through thy name will we tread them under that rise up against us. For I will not trust in my bow, neither shall my sword save me. In God we boast all the day long.* Others that have heard, will say, such and such an one was thus exercised, and God appeared for them, and put songs of praise to the Lord into their mouths; we will commit our case to God too; we will both hope and quietly wait for God's salvation too. Your telling others, how you have found God a prayer-hearing God, will encourage them, prayer-wise, to be committing their distresses and difficult cases to him. What an honour to be instrumental to any soul's comfort, and God's honour; agreeable to this is that Psal. lxxviii. 5, 6, 7. *Which he commanded our fathers,*

fathers, that they should make them known to their children: That the generation to come might know them, even the children which should be born; who should arise and declare them to their children: That they might set their hope in God, and not forget the works of God; but keep his commandments.

6th Reason. Because the works of God towards them have been very wonderful. The psalmist often speaks of the works of God as marvelous; they are wonderful, if we consider how God timed the mercy; when their feet well nigh slipt, when they could see no way of escape; as with the children of Israel at the Red Sea. How very wonderful and marvellous was the work of God, in putting by the wicked purpose of Haman against Mordecai and the Jews? If we consider how God kept from falling, by making them pass a right judgment on their ways and his ways, as Psal. lxxiii. Yea, appearing to save them, when with Jonah they were saying, *They were cast out of God's sight.* All refuge seemed

to

to fail, none shewing any care for their soul;
even then God made good his word, on which
he had caused them to hope, as Psalm cxlii.
per totum. The works of God are marvellous, if we consider the way and manner of
ushering in the mercy, the instruments that
were made use of, and how he disappointed
the counsels of the crafty.

7th Reason. Because it is a good evidence,
that they regarded and took notice of the
works of God in mercy, and would not forget his wonderful works towards them. For
hereby they put others under advantages to
put them in mind what favours they have
received from God.

Use I. Of Instruction. And, First, It
informs us that it is very acceptable to God, for
Christians to entertain the report of the experiences of others, to excite their own hearts to
glorify God. For if God make it a duty in
the receiver to report, it lays the hearer under
an obligation to set such remarks upon the
passages of divine providence to others, as
                                        may

may be useful to engage their hearts to glorify
God, for the favours and blessings he has
bestowed upon others.   And therefore, in obedience to God's command, that you may
be under advantages to glorify God, I will
now make a report of some of the great things
God has done for those you have been putting up so many prayers to God for.   God
has eminently been fufilling that word, Psalm
cvi. 46.   *He made them also to be pitied, of
all those that carried them captives.*

God hath made those whose characters
have been, that they were such whose tender mercies were cruelties; such from whom
one act of pity and compassion could scarce be
expected, even such who have delighted in
cruelty; to pity and compassionate such who
were led into captivity by them.   Made them
bear on their arms, and carry on their shoulders, our little ones, unable to travel.   Feed
their prisoners with the best of their provision: Yea, sometimes pinch themselves, as to
their daily food, rather than their captives.

To

To pity them under sickness, and afford all
proper means for the restoration of their
health, or recovery from lameness. Made
heathen's bowels yearn towards poor infants
exposed to death, so as to work out their
deliverance from fatal strokes, by burdening
of themselves. Oh! let us adore the riches
of the grace of God, who in wrath remembers
mercy, and doth not stir up all his wrath;
and from hence be encouraged, when under
convictions of God's being angry with us,
yet to look to him for mercy.

God has upheld many poor souls under all
manner of disadvantages, as to getting of
knowledge, and kept them from falling,
though crafty adversaries were under all advantages, and painful endeavours used to
seduce them. Being without Bibles, ministers, or Christian friends to confer with, daily
harrassed with temptations and tempters :
Some threatened, some flattered, some shut
up and confined in monasteries, where no
means were unessayed to gain them to change
their religion.   God

God has strengthened them to go through tedious journeys, and renewed strength, when they were even fainting in their spirits; thinking it not possible to travel five miles, and yet enabled to travel at least forty in a day. Remarkably ordering seasons, so as to be for their comfort in their travels; causing a moist snow to fall on the lake, only to such a height as to make it easy to their swoln and wounded feet: Changing the winds for their advantages, in petty voyages, in their ticklish canoes.

They have found God a little sanctuary to them, in the land of strangers; even there they have found the consolations of God through Christ not to be small; so that some of the most joyful and refreshing favours from heaven, have been given in to their souls, when under all sorts of outward afflictions.

They have found God a God hearing prayers, when they have gone to him with their most difficult cases, preserving them from falling; recovering theirs from falls; to making void the counsels of adversaries, disappointing

disappointing them in the things they dealt most proudly in. God has brought his to a resignation to his will, and then appeared dealing out mercies, as the very case did require.

God has sanctified to some, their former Sabbath solemn attendances on duties of piety, private as well as publick; and a religious education to be an unanswerable objection against such who were zealous for the traditions of men, to a visible profaning God's Sabbaths. They durst not embrace that religion, whose principles as well as practices, were so contrary to the precepts of God's holy word. Oh ! how should ministers and parents be encouraged from hence to use their utmost care, that God's Sabbaths may be duly sanctified by all under their charge; and that they would be exemplary before others, in a due observance of holy time.

God has made the falls of some to popery a means for the recovery of others; and making those things, by which the adversary
thought

thought to increase their numbers and proselytes, to be occasional of recovering such who
from their youth had been educated in the
popish way; having been taken captives when
young. Do not be discouraged, and say,
your friends and relations have (being captivated when young) for a long time lived in
popery, and therefore no hopes of recovery;
for God can make dry bones, very dry, to live,
and can in ways unthought of by you, both
recover them after they have fallen, and return
them again. The adversaries have sometimes pretended miracles for the confirmation
of their religion, that they might seduce
to popery; in fallacious ways caused reports that some captives died papists; that
one appeared in flames of fire to bear a tes-
timony against the Protestant religion; but
God has, in his wise providence, made known
their falsehoods and lies.

They have sought to persuade some, by
sums of money, to change their religion, offering honour and advancement to them at the
same

same time; but God has enabled them to resist and hate such allurements.

The reading the fourth chapter of Deuteronomy, a means of recovering one from popery.

God has made some, with an heroical, yea with a right Christian courage, to welcome death. Oh let every one get such a preparedness for death, that a sudden death may not be a terror!

God has made some, by the want of sanctuary mercies, to set an higher value upon the ordinances of Jesus Christ. Oh learn to prize and improve them, lest God teach you, by the briars and thorns of the wilderness, the worth of them, and make you weep when you sit down at the rivers of Babylon.

God has strengthened some to stand, when they have not only been threatened with all cruelties if they refused, but when the hatchet has been lifted up, with a threatening of speedy death in case of refusal. Oh let every one trust in God, who is a seasonable help and a present refuge!   INSTRUCTION

INSTRUCTION II. How they are to blame, that do not regard and take notice of the works of God, nor treasure up the remembrance of them in their minds. How soon are mercies like to be forgotten; the psalmist says, *Forget not all his benefits.* It was the great sin of the Israelites of old, that they soon forgat God's wondrous works. The holy God gave order, that his people should erect stones of remembrance, that his wonderful works of mercy to his people might not be forgotten; yea, commanded parents to tell their children, from generation to generation, what great things he had done for them. How are they then to blame that say, *They bless God for their mercies,* and do not rehearse the praise-worthy works of divine providence to others.

USE II. To direct such, who have received great and eminent mercies from God, in this way of making known to others the wonders of mercy to them, to be praising God. It is one way very proper and agreeable to the

revealed,

revealed will of God: You must watch against all vain ostentation.

USE III. Of EXHORTATION. To all who have, in a more peculiar way and manner, been casting off the effects and fruits of divine bounty and goodness, to be declaring what great things God has done for them. Therefore, 1. Beware of all manner of pride. Sometimes men cannot declare the great works of God done for them, without making known their own weakness, and therefore are silent, and hold their peace; they had rather God should lose his glory, than they any of their credit or esteem. But the holy psalmist says, *His feet had well nigh slipt*; yea, *that in his haste he had said, all men are liars;* and that one day he should surely perish; take shame to himself, that he might magnify the preventing and delivering grace and goodness of God. Sometimes men's pride makes them so admire their own parts and contrivances, as to over-look the works of divine providence; they sacrifice to their own net,

net, and burn incense to their own drag; and
say they have so much learning and knowledge, that they could easily answer arguments
to seduce them to popery; and so do not see
and acknowledge the goodness of God, in
preserving and keeping them.

2. Beware of a stupid, senseless, sloth-
ful spirit. The works of God are sought out
of them that have pleasure in them. Some
will not be at the pains to recollect the passages of divine providence; will not commit
them to writing, or to their memories, and
therefore soon forget them; they never wisely
observe the heightening circumstances of their
mercies.

Consider, 3. How heavenly an employ
and service it is, to be glorifying and praising
God. It will be one part of the work of
heaven, to be telling of the wonderful works
of God towards us. Begin such an heavenly
employ on earth. Hereby you will also interest yourselves in the prayers of others: To
have many prayers going daily to God for
                                              you,

you, how great a favour is it ! Others hearing
what mercies you have had, will bear you upon
their hearts when at the throne of grace, that
you may suitably improve such mercies.

The glorifying God is the greatest and chiefest concern of gracious souls; and the glorifying of God here, is the way to be glorified
by, and with God forever. The not glorifying God is very displeasing to him, and a way
to deprive ourselves of the sweet and comfort of our mercies. God accounts forgetting
of mercies, a forgetting himself.

END OF THE SERMON.

APPENDIX.

Drawn up and sent to the Rev. Mr. PRINCE, *by the Rev. Mr.* STEPHEN WILLIAMS, *of Springfield, who on February 29th, 1703-4, was, with his Rev. father, Mr.* JOHN WILLIAMS, *of Deerfield, carried captive into Canada, but returned, and was educated at Harvard College.*

Names of those Persons who were taken Captive at Deerfield, Feb. 29th, 1703-4.

MARY Alexander,
Mary Alexander, jun.
Joseph Alexander, *ran away the first night.*
Sarah Allen,
Mary Allis,
Thomas Baker,
Simon Beaumont,
Hannah Beaumont,
* Hephzibah Belding,
John Bridgman, *ran away in the meadow.*
Nathaniel Brooks,
* Mary Brooks,
† Mary Brooks, jun.
† William Brooks,
Abigail Brown,
Benjamin Burt,
John Burt,
Sarah Burt,
* Hannah Carter,
* Hannah Carter, jun.
† Mercy Carter,
† Samuel Carter,
† John Carter,
Ebenezer Carter,
* Marah Carter,
John Catlin,
Ruth Catlin,
* Elizabeth Corse,
† Elizabeth Corse, jun.
† Daniel Crowfoot,
† Abigail Denio,
Sarah Dickinson,
Joseph Eastman,
Mary Field,
John Field,
† Mary Field, jun.
* Mary Frary,
Thomas French,

* Mary French,
Thomas French, jun.
Mary French, jun.
† Freedom French,
† Martha French,
† Abigail French,
† Mary Harris,
† Samuel Hastings,
* Elizabeth Hawks,
Mehuman Hinsdel,
Mary Hinsdel,
Jacob Hix, *died at Cowass.*
Deacon David Holt, *died at Cowass.*
Abigail Holt,
Jonathan Holt,
Sarah Holt,
† Ebenezer Holt,
* Abigail Holt, jun.
Elizabeth Hull,
† Thomas Hurst,
† Ebenezer Hurst,
* Benoni Hurst,
Sarah Hurst,
Sarah Hurst, jun.
Elizabeth Hurst,
† Hannah Hurst,
Martin Kellogg,
Martin Kellogg, jun.
Joseph Kellogg,
† Joanna Kellogg,
Rebecca Kellogg,
John Marsh,
Sarah Muttoon,
* Philip Muttoon,
* Frank, *a negro.*
* Mehitable Nims,
Ebenezer Nims,
† Abigail Nims,

Joseph Petty,
Sarah Petty,
Lydia Pomroy,
Joshua Pomroy,
* Esther Pomroy,
Samuel Price.
† Jemima Richards,
† Josiah Riseing,
Ebenezer Shelden,
Remembrance Shelden,
Mary Shelden,
John Stebbins,
Dorothy Stebbins,
John Stebbins, jun.
Samuel Stebbins,
† Ebenezer Stebbins,
† Joseph Stebbins,
† Thankful Stebbins,
† Elizabeth Stevens,
Ebenezer Warner,
* Waitstill Warner,
† Waitstill Warner, jun.
Sarah Warner,
Rev. John Williams,
* Mrs. Eunice Williams,
Samuel Williams,
Stephen Williams,
† Eunice Williams, jun.
Esther Williams,
Warham Williams,
John Weston,
Judah Wright,
Three Frenchmen who had lived in the town for some time, and came from Canada, were also taken.

NOTE. Where there is this sign * against the person's name, it is to signify they were killed after they went out of town: And this mark † is to signify that they are still absent from their native country.

Names

Names of those who were slain at that time in or near the town.

SLAIN IN THE TOWN.

DAVID Alexander,
Thomas Carter,
John Catlin,
Jonathan Catlin,
Sarah Field,
Samson Frary,
John French,
Alice Hawks,
John Hawks, jun.,
    and his wife
Thankful Hawks,
John Hawks,
Martha Hawks,

Samuel Hinsdale,
Joseph Ingersol,
Jonathan Kellogg,
Philip Matloon's wife
    and child,
Parthena, *a negro.*
Henry Nims,
Mary Nims,*
Mercy Nims,
,Mehitable Nims,
Sarah Price,
Mercy Root,
Thomas Shelden,

Mrs. Shelden,
Mercy Shelden,
Samuel Smead's wife and
    two children,
Elizabeth Smead,
Martin Smith,
Serg. Benoni Stebbins,
Andrew Stevens,
Mary Wells,
John Williams, jun.
Jerusha Williams.

SLAIN IN THE MEADOW.

SAMUEL Allis,
Serg. Boltwood,
Robert Boltwood,

Joseph Catlin,
Samuel Foot,
David Holt, jun.

Jonathan Ingram,
Serg. Benjamin Wait,
Nathaniel Warner.

* These three it was supposed were burnt in the cellar.

An account of the mischief done by the enemy in Deerfield from the beginning of its settlement to the death of the Rev. Mr. JOHN WILLIAMS, *in June,* 1729.

1. T H E enemy beset the place, and killed one James Egleston, September 1, 1675.

2. The Indians fell upon the people as they were going to public worship, on Sept. 12, 1675, and wounded one Samuel Harrington in the neck, but the wound did not prove mortal. One man was drove into the swamp, taken and killed.

3. Captain Lothrop and company were slain at Muddy brook (alias) Bloody brook, on Sept. 18, 1675.

4. The

4. The *fall fight* (as it is called) was on May 18, 1676, when a great slaughter was made of the enemy, but Capt. Turner and 37 men were lost. There were many remarkables, relating to this affair, (as related by Jonathan Wells, Esq., who was present) which are not taken notice of by Mr. Hubbard or Dr. Mather.

5. Sept. 19, 1677. John Root was killed, and Serg. Plympton, Quintin Stockwell, and Benoni Stebbins, were taken captive, but Stebbins made his escape from them and got home. This was after they began to settle the place a second time; for upon Capt. Lothrop's loss, the town was deserted for some time; but this year, 1677, they began to build again. Serg. Plympton was accounted a gracious man; he was burnt by the Indians, and the Indians obliged one Dickinson, taken at Hatfield, to lead him to the stake: The manner of burning was this; they covered him with dry bark, set it on fire, then they quenched the fire, and anon firing it again. He went cheerfully to the stake, &c. The town was deserted for some time: In 1684, they returned again to settle the town.

6. June 1693. The widow Hepzibah Wells and her three daughters were knocked on the head and scalped, two of them died, but the other lived; at.the same time Thomas Broughton was killed, and his wife, great with child, and three of their children.

7. On October 13, 1693. Martin Smith was taken, and

and carried to Canada, from whence he returned after
some years.

8. Sept. 15, 1694. Monsieur Castreen, with a number
of Indians, beset the fort, but were beat off: Daniel Severance (a lad) was killed in the meadow; and John
Beaumont, and Richard Lyman, soldiers in the fort,
were wounded, but recovered. Mrs. Hannah Beaumont
and some children who were her scholars, were remarkably preserved: As they ran from the house to the fort,
the enemy fired many shot at them, and the bullets
whistled about their ears; but none of them were hurt,
although some of the enemy were very near them.

9. August 18, 1695. Mr. Joseph Barnard was fired
upon by the enemy, and his horse was shot down: He
himself was wounded in the body, one wrist shivered to
pieces, his other hand wounded; but yet through the
bravery of Godfry Nims, and others with him, he was
brought into the town, and lived till Sept. 6, and then died,
greatly lamented, &c.

10. Sept. 16, 1696. John Gillet and John Smead, were
hunting up Green river; the Indians came upon them,
and took Gillet, but Smead made his escape; the enemy
left two or three men with Gillet, and the rest came
along to the town, and assaulted Daniel Belding's house,
took Mr. Belding, his son Nathaniel, and daughter
Esther, captive: Killed his wife and three children, and
wounded Samuel and Abigail, but they recovered,
                                              although

although Samuel had a hatchet stuck in his head, and some of his brains came out at the wound.

11. July, 1698. Nathaniel Pomroy was killed, being with a party of men that went up the river after some Indians that had done mischief at Hatfield: At the same time Samuel Dickinson, and one —— Charly, were retaken from the enemy. This is related by Dr. Cotton Mather, in his history of the ten years war, &c.

12. October 8, 1703. Zebediah Williams and John Nims, were taken captive, and carried to Canada; Williams died there; Nims, with some others, made their escape, and got home to Deerfield, in 1705.

13. The town was taken February 29, 1703,4.

14. May 11, 1704. John Allen and his wife were killed at a place called the Barrs.

15. Serg. John Hawks, riding on the road, was fired at by the enemy, and wounded in the hand, but got off to Hatfield, and his wound was healed, &c. This was in the summer of 1704.

16. July 19, 1704. Thomas Russell was killed by the enemy, north of the town.

17. August, 1708. A scout went up to the white river, and as they returned, were fired upon by the enemy, and one man, whose name was Barber, was killed; and he killed the Indian that killed him. Martin Kellogg, jun. was taken captive, and the rest escaped.

18. Oct.

18. Oct. 26, 1708. E. Field was killed near muddy brook.

19. Mehuman Hinsdale was taken captive as he was driving his team from Northampton. This was April 11, 1709: The second time of his captivity: He was carried to Canada, and from thence to France, and got to England, and from thence home, &c.

20. May, 1709. Lieut. John Wells, and John Burt, were lost in a skirmish with the enemy on the French river, after they had been, with others, as far as Lake Champlain, and killed some of the enemy.

21. Joseph Clesson and John Arms were taken June 22, 1709, and the next day Jonathan Williams was killed, and Matthew Clesson mortally wounded; and Lieut. Thomas Taylor and Isaac Matloon were wounded, but recovered.

22. July 30, 1712. Serg. Samuel Taylor, and others, were sent out as a scout to the north river, they were attacked by the enemy, and Samuel Andross was killed; Jonathan Barrett was wounded in the side, and then taken; one William Sandford was also taken, the rest got home, &c. The prisoners were carried to Canada, where they met Lieut. Samuel Williams, who was then at Canada with a flag of truce), who ransomed them from the Indians, and brought them home: They were absent but about two months.

23. June 27, 1724. Ebenezer Shelden, Thomas Colton,

Colton, and Jeremiah English, (a friend Indian), were killed on the road beyond the green river houses; and it was supposed the enemy received some damage from some of our forces, who came upon them speedily, &c.

24. July 10, 1724. Lieut. Timothy Childs and Samuel Allen, were shot upon and wounded, as they were returning from their labour in the field, but they escaped, and were healed of their wounds.

25. August 25, 1725. Deacon Field, deacon Childs, and others, were going up to green river farms, and were ambushed by the Indians, but they discovered the Indians; and John Wells discharged his gun at an Indian, who fell: The Indians fired at them, and wounded deacon Samuel Field, the ball passing through the right hypocondria, cutting off three plaits of the mysenteria, which hung out of the wound, in length almost two inches, which was cut off even with the body, the bullet passing between the lowest and the next rib, cutting, at its going forth, the lowest rib: His hand being close to the body when the ball came forth, it entered at the root of the heel of the thumb, cutting the bone of the fore finger, and, resting between the fore and second finger, was cut out, and all the wounds were cured in less than five weeks, by doctor Thomas Hastings.

APPENDIX.

By the Rev. JOHN TAYLOR, *the present minister of the Gospel in Deerfield; containing some account of the mischief done by the enemy, in Deerfield, and its vicinity, from the death of the* Rev. Mr. WILLIAMS, *to the conclusion of the last French war.*

THE readers of this appendix, will probably feel desirous of knowing the reasons, why, in many things, I have been so general; only having given a brief statement of facts; and in others, have been more particular. I trust, it will be a sufficient apology to observe, that I have done it for want of better documents. Most of the facts mentioned, I have taken from the minutes of some gentlemen, who kept them, only for their own satisfaction, and were not particular; and now, the distance of time, precludes the possibility of obtaining such an account of circumstances, as may be depended on.

One reason, of my adding this appendix, is, I suppose that it will not be disagreeable to any who were desirous that the narrative should be reprinted, especially the descendants of those who were either killed, wounded, or captivated; and for this reason I have been careful also to mention the names of such.

Another reason is, I think that every vestige of history, which respects the early settlement of a country, should be preserved, for the satisfaction of future generations.

THE

THE last account of mischief, mentioned in the former appendix, done by the enemy in this part of the country, was in August, 1725. This year, terminated the war. A treaty of peace was held at Boston, by commissioners from the General Court, and the chiefs of the Indian tribes; at which, articles were signed, and a long peace ensued.

There appeared, for many years, an unusually pacific spirit among the Indians; probably in consequence of some acts of the General Court, favourable to them in their trade. It was thought, that they never again would have been disposed to hostilities, had they not been under the immediate influence of French interest.

War was declared between France and England, March, 1744. The first year of the war, no Indians made their appearance in this part of the country: They had found by experience, that to maintain an open trade with the English, was greatly for their interest; and consequently at first, entered into the war with reluctance.

The first mischief that I can obtain an account of, done by the enemy, in this part of the country, in the course of this war, was in July, 1745; when a few Indians came to a place called the great meadow, about 16 miles above fort Dummer, on Connecticut river; two of whom, captivated William Phips, as he was hoeing his corn. After having taken, and led him about half a mile, they made a stand; and as the Indians afterwards informed, one of them

them having laid down his gun, and gone a few rods, for the purpose of fetching something he had left, on his return, Phips took up the Indian's gun, fired upon, and killed him; then fell upon the other with his hoe, struck him down, and bruised him, until he supposed he was dead; he then attempted to make his escape, but unfortunately, three more of the enemy came upon him, and killed him.

The same month, deacon Josiah Fisher, was killed, and scalped at a place called the upper Ashwelot.

October 11. The fort at the great meadow, was attacked by a large party of French and Indians; the attack was bold, and furious, but without success. No lives were lost. Nehemiah Howe was taken captive, and carried to Quebec, where he soon died. The enemy on their return, met one David Rugg, with another person, passing down Connecticut river in a canoe; Rugg they killed, and scalped, the other person, with some difficulty, made his escape.

I can find no farther account of mischief done by the enemy, in this part of the country, in the year 1745, but in '46 they began in season, and the sufferings of the people were very considerable.

In April, the enemy made their appearance at No. 4, (now Charleston), which was then the most northern settlement, on Connecticut river; Capt. John Spafford, Isaac Parker, and Stephen Farnsworth, being at a little

distance

distance from the fort, were captivated, and carried to Canada.

The same month, a party of Indians ambushed the road, between Northfield and Lunenburgh, and killed Joshua Holton.

On the 23d of the same month, a large party of the enemy, came to the upper Ashwelot, with a design to have taken the fort by surprise, but being discovered by a person who was providentially at that time at a little distance from the garrison, they were disconcerted; an action however ensued, which continued for some time; the enemy finally withdrew. In this action, John Bullard was killed, Nathan Blake was captivated, and the wife of Daniel M'Kinne, being out of the fort, was overtaken and stabbed. Before the enemy retired, they burnt several buildings, which was supposed to have been done, not so much for the sake of mischief, as to conceal their dead; there being many human bones afterwards found among the ashes.

In the beginning of May, the enemy again appeared at No. 4; a few people were near a barn, about sixty rods from the fort, when they were fired upon by a considerable body who had concealed themselves in the barn. Seth Putnam, a soldier belonging to the fort, was killed; whilst the enemy were endeavouring to scalp him, Major Willard, commander of the garrison, with two soldiers, ran near to them undiscovered, and fired upon them,

upon

upon which they retreated with great haste. The Indians afterwards reported to the prisoners in Canada, that at this time two of their number were mortally wounded, and died soon after.

May 6, a large party of Indians made an attempt upon the fort at Falltown; (now Bernardston), a person about forty rods from the fort discovering them, gave information to another farther distant than himself; by this the enemy found they were discovered, and ran immediately to the fort; an attack commenced, which continued for some time, and though there were but three soldiers in the fort, they defended it till the enemy withdrew. John Burk was slightly wounded, one house was burnt, and about ten cattle were killed. Two Indians were mortally wounded, who died soon after their return.

On the same day, Serg. John Hawks, and John Miles, were fired upon by two Indians, as they were riding out from fort Massachusetts, and were both wounded: Miles made his escape to the fort; Hawks fought for some time, and as afterwards appeared, might have taken them both prisoners had he understood their language; they asked him for quarter before he turned to make his escape.

10th. Five of that party of Indians, who the day before had been at Falltown fort, ambushed the road at Colrain. Matthew Clark, with his wife and daughter, together with two soldiers were fired upon, a few rods from the fort; Clark was killed, and his wife and daughter were wounded;

wounded; one of the soldiers returning the fire, killed one of the enemy, which gave them a check, and he brought the wounded into the fort.

A few days after, about twenty men were out, fifty or sixty rods from the fort, at No. 4, viewing the place where Parker was killed on the 2d of the month, and before they discovered an enemy, they were fired upon by a large body of Indians, who immediately endeavoured to cut off their communication with the fort; Capt. Stevens, commander of the garrison, came out with a body of men for their relief, a severe action commenced, which continued for some time; at last the enemy fled; and as was supposed with considerable loss. Capt. Stevens lost three, viz. Aaron Lyon, Peter Perrin, and Joseph Marcy; he had four wounded, and one taken captive.

June 11. A party of the enemy again appeared at fort Massachusetts; a number of men being at some distance from the fort, were attacked, and a skirmish ensued: The enemy fled, after sustaining the fire but a few moments. Elisha Nims, and Gershom Hawks were wounded; and Benj. Tenter was captivated. One of the enemy was killed.

19th. A large body of the enemy again appeared at No. 4; Capt. Stevens, and Capt. Brown, marching with about fifty men from the fort into the meadow, were ambushed; the enemy were discovered before they fired: Stevens began the attack, and a severe action ensued; after some
time

time the enemy were repulsed, and retreated in great haste and confusion. Capt. Stevens lost none on the spot. Jedediah Winchel was mortally wounded, and died soon after. David Parker, Jonathan Stanhope, and Noah Heaton were also wounded, but recovered.

20th. A party of about twenty Indians came to Bridgman's fort, about two miles below fort Dummer, and fell upon a number of men who were at work in the meadow. In this skirmish William Robins and James Parker were killed; John Beaumont and Daniel How were taken captive; M. Gilson, and Patrick Ray were wounded, but recovered.

July 3. The enemy waylaid a mill in Hinsdale; Colonel Willard having come to the mill with a guard of about 20 men, for the purpose of grinding, and having placed his guards, they were soon fired upon; the Col. calling to his men with great earnestness to fall upon them, gave them such a fright, that they fled, leaving behind them their packs, and provisions, to the value of 40l. old tenor.

28th. David Morrison, of Colrain, was taken captive, near one of the garrisons.

August 3. A body of the enemy appeared at No. 4; suspicions of their approach were excited by the yelling of dogs. A scout was sent out from the fort, and had proceeded but a few rods before they were fired on. Ebenezer Philips was killed; the remainder made their escape to the fort; the enemy surrounded the garrison, and endeavoured,

endeavoured, for three days, to take it; but finding their efforts ineffectual, they withdrew, after having burnt several buildings, and killed all the cattle, horses, &c. which they could find.

11th. Benj. Wright, of Northfield, riding in the woods, was fired on, and mortally wounded; he died in a few hours.

17th. Ezekiel Wallingford was killed, and scalped, at a place called Poquiag. The same day, a person by the name of Bliss, was killed, and scalped, on the road between Deerfield, and Colrain, or Bernardston.

20th. An army of about nine hundred French and Indians, under command of Gen. de Vaudreuil, made an attack upon fort Massachusetts. The fort was commanded by Col. Hawks, who, unfortunately, was not in a situation to defend it against such a force, having but thirty-three persons, men, women, and children, in the fort; and being miserably provided with ammunition; with great fortitude, he defended it for twenty-eight hours; and had not his ammunition failed, it is probable he never would have given up the fort. He was, finally, necessitated to capitulate; and he offered such articles as were accepted by de Vaudreuil. One special article in this capitulation, was, that none of the prisoners should be delivered into the hands of the Indians; the next day, however, Vaudreuil divided the prisoners, and delivered them one half, in open violation, and contempt of the article.

article.* The Indians immediately killed one, who, by reason of sickness, was unable to travel. The prisoners were, in general, treated with civility, most of whom were afterwards redeemed. Col. Hawks lost but one man in the siege. Gen. de Vaudreuil, according to the best accounts the prisoners could obtain, lost forty-five, who were either killed outright, or died of their wounds.

Immediately, after the capture of the fort, a party of about fifty Indians came on, for the purpose of making depredations upon Deerfield. They came first upon a hill, at the south west corner of the south meadow, where they discovered ten, or twelve, men and children at work, in a situation, in which they might all, with ease, be made prisoners. Had they succeeded in their design, which was, to obtain prisoners, rather than scalps, it is probable that events would not have been so disasterous as they proved. They were disconcerted by the following circumstance: Mr. Eleazer Hawks was out that morning a fowling, and was providentially at the foot of the hill, at the time the enemy came down; they, seeing him, supposed they were discovered, and immediately fired upon him, killed, and scalped him. This gave an alarm to the people in the meadow, some of whom were but a few rods

---

* General de Vaudreuil's plea for this breach of faith, was, the danger of mutiny in his army, the Indians being irritated to a great degree, on account of their being cut off, by the capitulation, from all the profits of the conquest. But, how far this plea was a justification of such perfidy, I leave to the judicious to determine.

rods distant. The enemy were now sensible, that what
they did must be done with dispatch. Accordingly they
rushed into the meadow, fired on Simeon Amsden, a lad,
and killed him, beheaded, and scalped him. Mr. Samuel Allen, John Sadler, and Adonijah Gillet, ran a few
rods, and made a stand, under the bank of the river,
where they were attacked with fury, and fought for a
little time with great bravery; they were, however, soon
overpowered with numbers. Allen and Gillet fell. Sadler, finding himself alone, ran across the river, and made
his escape, amidst a shower of balls. Whilst this was
passing, Oliver Amsden was pursued a few rods, overtaken, and stabbed, after having his hands and fingers
cut in pieces, by endeavouring to defend himself against
the enemies' knives. At the same time, three children
by the name of Allen, all of whom are still living, were
pursued; Eunice, one of the three, was struck down with
a tomahawk, which was sunk into her head, but by reason of the haste in which the enemy retreated, she was
left unscalped, and afterwards recovered. Caleb, the
present Mr. Caleb Allen, of Deerfield, made his escape;
and Samuel was taken captive, the only prisoner who
was taken at this time.* The firing immediately alarmed
the

* This lad, after a year and nine months, was redeemed. Col.
Hawks, who was sent to Canada for the purpose of redeeming
captives, after enquiring for the lad, was informed, that he was
unwilling to be seen, and that he expressed great dissatisfaction
upon hearing of his arrival: When he was brought into the
presence of Col. Hawks, he was unwilling to know him, although

the town. Capt. Hopkins, commander of the standing guard, together with most of the inhabitants, as volunteers, came on with the utmost expedition, but the enemy had withdrawn in great haste, expecting, no doubt, a violent attack; they were pursued several miles by a body of men, under the command of Capt. Clesson, but could not be overtaken.

It does not appear, as a matter of certainty, that more than one of the enemy was killed at this time, and him, by Samuel Allen; sometime after, however, the remains of a person were found, near the place of action, supposed to be those of an Indian.

This was the last mischief, done by the enemy, in the western frontiers, this season.

April 7, 1747. A large body of French, and Indians, appeared at No. 4, and laid siege to the garrison, which continued for three days, when the enemy withdrew, having done but little damage; only slightly wounding Joseph Ely, and John Brown,.

15th. Nathaniel Dickinson, and Asahel Burt, of Northfield,

he was his uncle, and had always been acquainted with him in Deerfield; neither would he speak in the English tougue, not that he had forgotten it, but to express his unwillingness to return; he made use of various arts, that he might not be exchauged; and finally could not be obtained but by threats, and was brought off by force. In this we see the surprising power of habit; this youth had lost his affection for his country, and his friends, in the course of one year, and nine months; and had become so attached to the Indians, and their mode of living, as that to this day, he considers that of the Indians, the happiest life. This appears more surprising when we consider, that he fared extremely hard, and was reduced almost to a skeleton.

field, being out a little distance from the town, were killed, and scalped. The enemy, on their return from North-field, burnt most of the buildings in Winchester, and in the upper, and lower Ashwelots, which plantations, a few days before, had been deserted by the inhabitants, not having sufficient protection afforded them by government.

May 25. As fort Massachusetts was rebuilding, there being several hundred people present, an army of the enemy came, with a design to hinder the undertaking. About an hundred men, a few days before, had been sent to Albany, for stores of provisions, and ammunition, being on their return, and near the fort, a scout was sent forward, who, coming within sight of the fort, discovered the enemy, and began an attack; this gave an alarm to the people at the fort, who, as yet, had not discovered the enemy; a few issued out, and maintained a small skirmish, till the enemy withdrew. There was, at the time, much complaint, both of the people at the fort, and of the commander of that party who was with the wag-gons, for not affording assistance, which was imputed to cowardice. In this action, three persons were wounded; and a friend Indian, who belonged to Stockbridge, was killed.

July 15. Eliakim Sheldon, of Bernardston, was fired upon, and wounded; he died the following night.

The same month, John Mills, of Colrain, passing from what was called the south fort, to his own house, was fired upon and killed.   August

August 26. A small party of the enemy came to a village belonging to Northampton, (now Southampton), and killed, and scalped, Elijah Clark, as he was threshing in his barn.

October 1. Peter Burvec was taken captive near Massachusetts' fort.

19th. John Smead, as he was travelling from Northfield to Sunderland, was killed, and scalped, near the mouth of Miller's river. He had but a few days before returned from captivity, being one who was taken at Massachusetts' fort, with his wife, and children.

About this time, Jonathan Sawtel, was taken captive, from Hinsdale.

14th. As twelve men were passing down the river, from No. 4, they were ambushed, and a skirmish ensued; Nathaniel Gould, and Thomas Goodall, were killed, and scalped; Oliver Avery was wounded, and John Henderson taken captive, the remainder made their escape.

March 15, 1748. About eight men were out a few rods from the fort, at No. 4, and were attacked by about twenty Indians, who endeavoured to cut off their retreat to the fort; a skirmish ensued, in which Charles Stevens was killed; a man by the name of Androus was wounded, and Eleazer Priest was taken captive.

April 12. Jason Babcock was taken prisoner, being at work in his field, at Poquiag.

May 9. Noah Pixley was killed, and scalped, at Southampton.   About

About the same time, Capt. Melvin, with eighteen men, being at the lake, near Crownpoint, fired at two canoes of Indians: On his return, being on West river, about 35 miles from fort Dummer, was ambushed, and being fired on by surprise, his men were scattered: Two or three returned the fire, and killed two of the enemy: The same persons, after having gone some distance, and having fallen in company with three or four of their own men, concluded to return back, and give the enemy a shot; on their return they were fired on, and one was killed; they returned the fire, and killed one of the enemy. The whole company, excepting six, made their escape through the woods, and came in at different times. In this skirmish, Joseph Petty, John Heywood, John Dod, Daniel Mann, and Isaac Taylor, were killed; Samuel Severance could not be found, and was supposed to be taken captive. The loss of these men, was much lamented; and they are spoken of with respect, as prudent, virtuous men, and resolute soldiers.

June 16. As thirteen men were marching from Colonel Hinsdale's, to fort Dummer, they were ambushed by a large body of the enemy and were fired upon. Joseph Richardson, Nathan French, and John Frost, were killed the first shot, and seven were immediately taken captive, viz. Henry Stevens, Benjamin Osgood, William Blanchard, Matthew Wiman, Joel Johnson, Moses Perkins, and William Bickford. Bickford was either killed by the enemy,

enemy, the first night, or had been wounded, and died of his wounds.

26th. Capt. Hobbs, passing through the woods from No. 4, to fort Shirley, with forty men, and being about twelve miles northwest of fort Dummer, was attacked by a large body of the enemy, who had pursued him; it being in the middle of the day, he had made a stand, that his men might receive some refreshment; whilst they were dining, the scout, which was sent upon the back track, were fired on. Upon this, Capt. Hobbs put his men into as much readiness for an action, as two or three minutes would admit of. The enemy came on with great fury, expecting, no doubt, an immediate surrendry; but Capt. Hobbs gave them a warm reception, and fought, for four hours, with such boldness and fortitude, as that had he, and his men, been Romans, they would have received a laurel, and their names would have been handed down with honour, to the latest posterity; the enemy finally fled in haste, and with great loss. Capt. Hobbs, in this action, lost but three men, and had but three wounded; those killed were Ebenezer Mitchel, Eli Scott, and Samuel Gunn.

July 14. As a scout of seventeen men were passing from Col. Hinsdale's to fort Dummer, they were ambushed, and fired upon, by about 120 of the enemy; two only were killed the first shot; two more were wounded, and but four made their escape; the remainder were taken

captive,

captive; the wounded the enemy killed, after having carried them about a mile.

23d. The enemy waylaid the main street, at Northfield, and killed Aaron Belding.

August 2. About 200 of the enemy, made their appearance at fort Massachusetts; the fort was then under the command of Capt. Ephraim Williams: A scout was first fired upon, which drew out Capt. Williams with about thirty men; an attack began, which continued for some time; but, finding the enemy numerous, Capt. Williams fought upon the retreat, till he had again recovered the fort: The enemy soon withdrew, and with what loss was unknown. In this action, one Abbot was killed, Lieut. Hawley, and Ezekiel Wells were wounded, but recovered.

This is the last account I can find, of mischief done by the enemy in the western frontiers, in what is called the first French war. Peace, however, was not finally settled with the Indians, until October, 1749, when a treaty was held at Falmouth, by commissioners from the General Court, and the chiefs of the Indian tribes, by whom a former treaty, with some additions, was renewed.

Peace between France and England, took place in the year 1748, and war was again declared in 1756; but, in the summer of '55, a body of Indians appeared at Stockbridge, killed several persons, and did considerable mischief, in killing cattle, &c.

In June, the same summer, a number of persons being
at

at work in the meadow, at the upper part of Charlemont, were fired on by a party of the enemy; not so much mischief was done, as might have been expected; a number made their escape: Cap. Rice, and Phinehas Arms, were killed, their bodies were afterwards found in a mangled condition. Titus King, and a lad, were taken captive.

The same month, Capt. Bridgman's fort, at Hinsdale, was taken by stratagem, and a number of persons were captivated. It was supposed that the enemy had been lurking about for some time, and the situation of the fort was such as that whatever passed, either in, or near it, might be easily seen from the hills a little back: It was the custom of the fort, for the women within to fasten the gate when the men went into the fields to labour, and to open it upon their return, from the signal of knocking: The Indians observing this, took an opportunity when the men were at the greatest distance from the fort, came, and knocked at the gate; and the women, being under no special apprehensions of an enemy, immediately threw open the gate, when, to their astonishment, they found the enemy entering; no resistance was made in the fort, and fourteen persons were taken captive. The enemy made no longer tarry at the fort, than to secure the prisoners, but rushed into the meadow, and fell upon the men, who, as yet, had not discovered what had passed at the fort; they made as much resistance as their situation would admit of. In this skirmish, C. Howe was killed, the remainder made their escape.   About

About this time, the fort at Keene, under the command of Capt. Sims, was attacked by a large party of Indians, and with great fury; the attack was lengthy, but was sustained with fortitude. The enemy finding their attempts to take the fort ineffectual, gave over the attack, but wreaked their vengeance on the inhabitants, by destroying all the property they could find, in killing cattle, burning buildings, &c. In this siege, no lives were lost, and but one person was taken captive, he being out of the fort at the time.

July 3. The enemy appeared at Keene, and captivated a person by the name of Frizzle.

The same month, fort Hinsdale was attacked by a considerable body of the enemy. In this attack two persons were killed, and one was taken captive; one of the persons killed was John Alexander.

About the same time, two men were killed, at Bellows's fort. Also, a man, by the name of Pike, was killed at some place up the river, but where I cannot tell.

June 7, 1756. Josiah Foster, with his family, were taken captive, at Winchester. The same day, a body of the enemy appeared at fort Massachusetts. Benjamin King, and a man by the name of Meacham, were killed.

The same month, Lieut. Joseph Willard, was killed at No. 4.

On the 25th, as a number of men were coming from the army at the lake, they were attacked by a large body
of

of the enemy, and it is probable that a severe action ensued, tho' I cannot ascertain the particulars; there were, however, eight men killed, and five taken captive.

July 11. The enemy came to West Hoosick, and killed Capt. Chapin, and two persons by the name of Chidester.

August 12, 1756. A party of five, or six Indians, made their appearance in Deerfield, (now Greenfield), at a place called the country farms; several men, viz. Benjamin Hastings, John Graves, Daniel Graves, Nathaniel Brooks, and Shubal Atherton, being at work, were surprised, by discovering the enemy between them and their guns, and being in no situation to make any resistance, found no way to save themselves, but by flight. They had fled but a few rods, before they were fired on; none were either killed, or wounded the first shot; the enemy still pursued, and continued their firing. Shubal Atherton was soon killed; Benjamin Hastings, and John Graves, made their escape; Daniel Graves, and Nathaniel Brooks, were taken captive. Graves was killed, after the enemy had conveyed him but a little distance; he was in years, and it was supposed, he was unable to travel with such speed as the enemy wished. Brooks never returned from his captivity.

1757. The enemy appeared at No. 4, and captivated five persons; the particulars of this matter I cannot ascertain.

March 20, 1758. J. Morrison, and J. Henry of Colrain,

rain, being near what is called north river, (a branch of Deerfield river), were fired on, and were both wounded; Capt. Morrison's barn was burnt, and his cattle were killed the same day.

March 21, 1759. The enemy again appeared at Colrain, and captivated Joseph M'Ewers, with his wife. Mrs. M'Ewers, was killed by the enemy, after one day's travel, she being unable to proceed.

This is the last account, which I can obtain, of mischief done by the enemy, in the western frontiers, in the last French war.

———————

APPREHENDING that it will not be disagreeable to the publick, I here subjoin a circumstantial account of what is called the *fall fight*, which happened in May, 1676.

The following, I have taken in part, from Hubbard's history of the Indian wars; but principally from an attested copy of a manuscript, written by some gentlemen who were in the action.

Several large bodies of Indians had assembled at different places about Deerfield. Two tribes had seated themselves at the falls, one on the east, and the other on the west side of the river. A little below the falls, upon an island, was another tribe. Another had placed themselves on the west side of the river, at a little distance
above

above the falls; And a fifth had taken their residence at Cheapside.

These Indians, being previously informed, by some of their captives, that the forces were principally withdrawn from the neighbouring towns, had imprudently fallen into a state of unguarded security. The inhabitants being informed of this, by some prisoners, who had been so fortunate as to make their escape, determined to improve the opportunity, and if possible, extirpate them from this part of the country. All the soldiers, who could be raised, for this almost desperate expedition, both from the militia, and the standing forces, amounted to only one hundred and sixty. The standing forces were commanded by Capt. Turner, of Boston. The volunteers by their own officers. Those from Springfield, by Capt. Holyoke; from Northampton, by Ensign Lyman; from Hadley, and Hatfield, by Sergeants Kellogg, and Dickinson. The Rev. Hope Atherton, minister of the gospel, at Hatfield, a gentleman of publick spirit, accompanied the army. The pilots were Messrs. Benjamin Wait, and Experience Hinsdale.

These troops marched from Hatfield, May 17, 1676, a little before night. Passing Deerfield river, at Cheapside, they were heard by the Indian sentinel, who immediately alarmed the tribe, informing them, that horses had passed the river. Search was immediately made, at the usual fording place, which our troops had happily missed, having

ing by mistake, crossed a little above, and the enemy
finding no tracks, concluded, that their sentry had been
deceived, and that what he heard, must have been the
noise of moose, passing the river near the fording place.
Meeting with no opposition from this tribe, our troops
marched on, till they came to the falls. It was now about
the break of day. According to their wishes, our army
found the enemy in an unguarded situation, without even
a sentinel. The reason why, at this time, they were thus
surprisingly unguarded, was, the evening before they
had been rioting upon milk, and roast beef, having been
pillaging cows from the neighbouring towns. When the
day opened, so that our army could distinguish friends
from foes, they marched up and began the attack, by
firing into the wigwams. The Indians awaking in
surprise, and in their consternation supposing that they
were attacked by their native enemies, cried, Mohawks!
Mohawks! They soon, however, discovered their mistake; but being in no situation to make an immediate
defence, great numbers were slain upon the spot, some,
in their surprise, ran directly into the river, and were
drowned; others betook themselves to their bark canoes,
and having in their confusion forgot their paddles, were
hurried down the falls, and dashed against the rocks;
and many who had endeavoured to secrete themselves
under the river banks, were discovered, and slain.

In this action the enemy, by their own confession, lost
300, women and children included.   This

This victory, though great, and obtained with the loss of only one man, in the first onset, was yet, however, disastrous in the issue. The few who had not been slain of this tribe, after recovering from their fright, and being joined by the neighbouring tribes, discovering the smallness of the number, by whom they had been thus furiously attacked, and by whom they had sustained such a loss, pursued, and harrassed the army on their retreat, with such fury, that thirty-seven were killed, and several were wounded.

This loss was imputed, in part, to the bodily infirmities of Capt. Turner; and in part, to the want of ammunition, which was the cause of an ill-timed and unguarded retreat.

A few, to the number of about twenty, did not quit the ground, with the main body of the army, but tarried behind, for the purpose of firing at some of the enemy who were crossing the river. These men soon found themselves under the necessity of disputing the ground, with a considerable body of the enemy, before they could recover their horses; but after a severe skirmish, obtained their object, and soon came up with the army, which was surrounded, and fought on their retreat for ten miles. Seven, or eight men, in the beginning of the retreat, were, by some accident, unfortunately separated from the army, and soon found themselves lost. The Indians afterwards gave the following account of them: That on
Monday

Monday after the fight, eight Englishmen came to them, who were lost, and offered to surrender, on condition their lives might be spared; but, instead of giving them quarter, they took and burnt them in the following manner:—They first covered them with dry thatch, then set fire to it, and compelled them to run: When one covering was burnt off, they put on another, and so continued till death delivered them from their hands.

This expedition was productive of very happy consequences, for the enemy were so disconcerted in all their plans, and so greatly disheartened, that they never after during that war, gave any considerable disturbance to the frontiers. From this expedition may be dated their decline in these parts.

In the above action was one Jonathan Wells, of Hatfield, then a youth in his 17th year, he was afterwards a gentleman improved in publick life, and sustained a worthy character. The following is the substance of an attested copy of the account, taken from his own mouth.

Mr. Wells was one of the 20 men abovementioned, who were under a necessity of disputing the ground, for the purpose of recovering their horses. Soon after he had mounted, being in the rear, three of the enemy fired upon him; one of their balls brushed his hair, another wounded his horse, and a third struck his thigh, in a place where it had before been broken with a cart wheel; the ball did not wholly break his thigh anew, but fractured the end of

one

one of the bones, which was a little projected over the
other, it having been badly set. Upon receiving the
wound, it was with difficulty that Mr. Wells kept in his
saddle. The Indians perceiving they had wounded him,
pressed hard upon him. Mr. Wells, recovering a little
from the first shock, and perceiving the enemy almost
upon him, presented his gun, which gave them a check,
and whilst they were charging, he made his escape, and
reached the company. He represented to Capt. Turner,
the danger to which the people in the rear were exposed,
and urged him to return to their relief, or halt till they
might come up; but he answered, "It is better to lose
some, than all." The army was now divided into several companies, one pilot crying, "If you will save your
lives, follow me;" and another, "If you regard your safety
follow me." Mr. Wells was now following a company,
whose course was towards a swamp; but perceiving that a
body of the enemy were there, he left that company, who
were all lost, and joined a small party, who were taking
a different route; but his horse soon failing by reason of
his wound, and himself being much weakened by loss
of blood, he was left by this party, having only one Jones,
a wounded man to accompany him: They had no path
to guide them, and were both unacquainted with the
woods. They had not travelled far, before Mr. Wells was
separated from Jones and finding himself faint, eat a nut-
meg which he had in his pocket, upon which he revived.
After

After having wandered in the woods for some time, he came upon green river, and he followed the course of it up, till he came to a place called the country farms; having passed the river he attempted to ascend a mountain on the west side, but fainted, and fell from his horse. How long he lay in this condition he knew not, but when he recovered, he found his horse standing by him, and his bridle hanging on his hand. He arose, tied his horse, and again laid himself down, but upon reflection, finding himself already so weak as to be unable to mount concluded that he should have no further use for his horse, and being unwilling that he should die at the tree, dismissed him; but unhappily forgot to take any provision from his portmanteau, although it contained a plenty. Towards night, being troubled with musquetoes, he struck up a fire; but this almost proved his destruction; it arose, and spread with such fury, among the leaves and trash, that it was with difficulty, in his faint condition, he escaped perishing in the flames. After he was out of danger, from the fire, he again laid himself down to rest; but now new fears arose; he imagined that the fire would direct the enemy where to find him; and serve to betray him into their hands: Unwilling the enemy should be benefitted by his ammunition, he cast it to as great a distance as he could, reserving only a charge or two for their use, should he fall into their hands. After some time, finding his fire had spread considerably, he took courage, put some

tow

tow into his wounds, bound them up with his handker-
chief, and composed himself to sleep. In his sleep he
dreamed, that his grandfather came to him, and told him
he was lost, and must turn, and go down that river, till
he should come to the end of a mountain, where he would
find a plain, upon which he must travel, in order to find
his way home. When he awoke he found himself refreshed, his bleeding stopped, and his strength recruited,
and with the help of his gun as a staff, he was able to
walk, though but slowly. The rising of the sun, con-
vinced him, he was lost, and that the course he intended
to pursue was wrong. He had now wandered six or
seven miles farther from home, than when he set out from
the place of action. And though, at first, he paid no
attention to his dream, now he determined to follow the
directions of it. Accordingly, he traveled down the river,
found the end of the mountain, and soon came to the
plain; all of which, agreed to the representation in his
dream.* Soon after he entered upon the plain, he found
a foot

* I doubt, whether, in this dream, there was any thing super-
natural, as some may be ready to suppose. Mr. Wells, having
wandered in the woods six or seven miles, must necessarily have
had some doubts whether his course was right; and his mind,
when asleep, would more naturally employ itself on this subject,
than any other; because to find the way home, must have been his
great object, when awake. His dreaming that his grandfather
appeared to him, was nothing strange; and his local situation at
this time was such, that he could not be entirely unacquainted
with the natural make of the ground; and his thoughts running as
they did, in this dream, would be natural; the river was near him
—the plain was before him—and the end of the mountain, near the
side of the plain, if he had not previously seen it, would naturally
be supposed.

a foot path, which led him to the road, in which, the
main body of the army returned. When he came to
Deerfield river, he met with much difficulty in crossing;
the stream carrying his lame leg across the other, so that
several of his first attempts were without effect. Finally,
however, with the help of his gun, with much difficulty he
reached the opposite shore. When he had ascended the
bank, being greatly fatigued, he laid himself down under
a walnut bush, and fell asleep. When he awoke, the
first object that presented, was an Indian in a canoe,
coming directly towards him. Mr. Wells now found
himself in a very unhappy condition, being so disabled
by his wounds that he could not flee, and his gun being
so filled with gravel and sand, in crossing the river, that
he could not fight. So soon however, as he perceived
the Indian had discovered him, he presented his gun,
which so affrighted him, that he leaped out of the canoe,
leaving his own gun, and made his escape. Mr. Wells
concluding that he would inform the whole tribe, who
were only a few rods distant, went into a neighbouring
swamp, and finding two logs lying near each other, and
covered with rubbish, he crept between them. He soon
heard the noise of Indians but was not curious to look out
after them. When the noise had ceased, he ventured to
proceed forward. In Deerfield meadow he found some
horses' bones, from which he scraped some matter,
which served for food; he also found two or three rotten
beans,

beans, where the Indians had threshed, and also two blue bird's eggs, which was all the sustenance he had till he reached home. He came to Deerfield town plat, on Saturday night about dark, but as there were no inhabitants present, the town having a little before been burnt, he continued his course in the evening.

He was often under great discouragements, and frequently laid himself down to die, expecting to rise no more. He reached no farther than muddy brook as the sun rose on Sabbath morning. Here, seeing a human head, which had been dug up by wild beasts, Mr. Wells, notwithstanding the distresses of his condition, stopped to find the grave, which having found he laid the head to the body, and covered it with billets of wood, to defend it from the ravenous beasts of the wilderness. After he had left the brook and entered upon the plain, he grew faint and very thirsty, but could obtain no water for a considerable time; he was, however, often refreshed, by holding his face in the smoke of burning knots of pine, which he frequently met with, as the woods were on fire. Mr. Wells arrived at Hatfield on the Sabbath, between meetings, and was received with inexpressible joy, as one having arisen from the dead. He endured incredible pain, and distress, with his wound, being confined several times to his bed, for six months together; and it was upwards of four years before he was sound.

In this action was also the Rev. Mr. Atherton, minister
of

of the gospel, in Hatfield. The following is the substance of a paragraph, which he delivered to his people the Sabbath after his return:

"In the hurry and confusion of the retreat, I was separated from the army; the night following, I wandered up and down among the dwelling places of the enemy, but none of them discovered me. The next day, I tendered myself to them a prisoner, for no way of escape appeared, and I had been a long time without food; but notwithstanding I offered myself to them, yet, they accepted not the offer; when I spake they answered not; and when I moved toward them they fled.* Finding they would not accept of me as a prisoner, I determined to take the course of the river and if possible find the way home, and after several days of hunger, fatigue and danger, I reached Hatfield."

Deerfield, October 10*th*, 1793.

* There were various conjectures at the time, relative to this strange conduct of the Indians; the most probable one was, that it arose from some of their religious superstitions.

The following observations were added by Mr. T. PRINCE, *to the third edition, for the information of our younger people.*

T H E reverend author of the preceeding history and sermon was a son of Mr. Samuel Williams, of Roxbury, where he was born Dec. 10, 1664; took his first degree at Harvard college in 1683; was ordained the first pastor of the church in Deerfield, in May, 1686.

And his first wife Eunice, murdered by the barbarous Indians, as before related, was the only daughter of the Rev. Mr. Eleazer Mather, first pastor of the church in Northampton, by his only wife, Mrs. Esther, the daughter of the reverend and famous Mr. John Warham, formerly a minister in Exeter, in England, who came to New-England in 1630, was the first teacher with the Rev. Mr. Maverick, pastor of the first church in Dorchester, near Boston; and in 1635, removed, with the greater part of his church, to Windsor, on Connecticut river, where he continued their pastor until he died. After the Rev. Mr. Eleazer Mather's death, his widow married the Rev. Mr. Solomon Stoddard, who succeeded him in the pastoral office at Northampton.

When Deerfield was destroyed, in February, 1703-4, it was in the first year of my living at Harvard college; and I well remember how generally and greatly affected were the good people of this province, with that terrible disaster.

His

His eldest son, Eleazer, being then in another town, escaped that calamity. The next commencement, by the encouragement and help of divers charitable people, especially in Boston, he entered Harvard college; and living in the chamber over me, I fell into an intimate acquaintance with him; and found him a person of eminent piety, humility, sincerity, and sweetness of temper, like his father. He took his first degree in 1708, and became the faithful pastor of the church in Mansfield in Connecticut, until he died.

His reverend father returning from captivity, and arriving at Boston, November 21, 1706, to the great joy of the people; and being informed that he was to preach the publick lecture there on December 6th, I, with many others, went down, and in an auditory exceedingly crowded and affected, I heard the sermon herewith reprinted. And in those times, there was such a tender union, affection, and Christian simplicity, among the good people here, that, as the apostle lively describes it, "When one member of the society suffered, the whole 'body seemed to suffer with it; and when one 'rejoiced, the whole rejoiced."

By the like kind encouragement, the Rev. Mr. Williams had his son Stephen Williams educated at Harvard college; who took his first degree in 1713; was ordained pastor of a church in Springfield; and is so extensively known and valued, that his name only needs to be mentioned;

as

as that of his son Warham—who took his first degree in
1719, and became the worthy pastor of the church in
Waltham, formerly a part of Watertown; not long since
deceased.

The Rev. Mr. Williams, of Deerfield, used every May,
yearly, to come down to the general convention of the ministers of the province at Boston; where he was always
very affectionately entertained.

At the convention in May, 1728, (being chosen the year
before) he preached a very moving sermon to the ministers; when I remember, he expressed his joy in the great
advantage we at that time had above the preceeding ministers, in the general awakenings through the land, by the
great earthquake in October foregoing.   And on June
12, 1729, he died, greatly beloved and lamented.

And by the accounts above, we may learn, from the
instance of this one town only in our western frontiers of
the province of the Massachusetts bay, in New-England,
what horrible murders and desolations this proivnce has
suffered from the French and Indians in all our wars
with them ever since the year 1675, when the Indians
first broke out upon us—and what numbers of the present
people in Canada are the children of this province, or
descendants from them—which, in case the sovereign
God should ever lead a victorious army of ours into Canada, will clearly justify us to all the world, if we should
bring every child and descendant of New-England, yea
                                                      of

of all the British colonies, away—especially considering we should bring them into a much pleasanter and more plenteous land and agreeable climate; out of a wretched land of darkness and slavery, both religious and civil, into a land of glorious light and liberty. And may the Almighty hasten it in his time!

T. Prince.

Boston, Dec. 20, 1757.

FINIS.

CPSIA information can be obtained
at www.ICGtesting.com
Printed in the USA
BVHW081735060222
628183BV00006B/287